AMSTERDAM

Published by Thomas Cook Publishing
PO Box 227, Thorpe Wood
Peterborough PE3 6PU
United Kingdom

E–mail: books@thomascook.com

Text: © The Thomas Cook Group Ltd 2000
Maps: © The Thomas Cook Group Ltd 2000
Transport map: © TCS 2000

ISBN 1 841570 338

Distributed in the United States of America by the Globe Pequot Press,
PO Box 480, Guilford, Connecticut 06437, USA.

Distributed in Canada by Whitecap Books, 351 Lynn Avenue,
North Vancouver, British Columbia, Canada V7J 2C4.

Distributed in Australia and New Zealand by Peribo Pty Limited,
58 Beaumont Road, Mt Kuring-Gai, NSW, 2080, Australia.

This edition published in the Netherlands, Belgium and Luxembourg by
Schuyt & Co, Postbus 563, 2003 RN Haarlem. ISBN 90 6097 550 2

Publisher: Stephen York
Commissioning Editor: Deborah Parker
Map Editor: Bernard Horton

Series Editor: Christopher Catling

Written and researched by: Paul Murphy

Cover photograph: Eddy Posthuma de Boer

must-see AMSTERDAM

PAUL MURPHY

GETTING TO KNOW AMSTERDAM

Getting
to know
Amsterdam

Discovering Amsterdam

Compared to London, Paris, Barcelona and most other major European cities, Amsterdam is just a large village. You can walk right across its centre in well under an hour, but to experience its myriad attractions might take you years.

Global village

In contrast to the dour northern image that the Netherlands conjures up, one of the most attractive features of Amsterdam is its cosmopolitan nature. Thanks to its maritime and trading prowess it became the world's market-place in the 17th century and today it remains an exotic haven for shopping and dining. Dive off the main canals into the narrow interconnecting side-streets and you'll find authentic Indonesian, French, Oriental, Middle Eastern and Mediterranean restaurants, alongside small, speciality shops dedicated to Indonesian artefacts, Spanish earthenware, Japanese antiques and Chinese furniture. And to make it all ridiculously easy almost everyone speaks perfect English.

Gezelligheid – or how to feel at home when you're away

There is no direct English translation for *gezellig* but comfy, cosy and convivial are all pretty close. Most brown cafés (*see page 174*) are very *gezellig*; McDonald's is about as un-*gezellig* as you can get. *Gezelligheid* (ie being *gezellig*) is also a state of mind; Amsterdammers chatting away or having a singsong in a Jordaan bar are usually very *gezellig*; drunken tourists on Rembrandtplein and Leidseplein are most definitely not.

The ultimate in *gezelligheid* is stumbling into a canalside brown café on a cold winter's day, striking up a conversation with a local, then warming body and soul with a bowl of thick *erwtensoep* (Dutch pea soup) washed down by a sweet dark *bokbier*. But that's just one opinion!

Sex and drugs and dog mess

There are two things that connect these three seemingly disparate Amsterdam strands: a) they are all conducted illegally on, or just off, the city streets; b) the city authorities, with the tacit approval of most Amsterdammers, turn a blind eye as long as they do not get out of hand. In Amsterdam

you can have your space cake and eat it, just watch where you're treading when you get outside. Of course, the argument against all this is that one man's freedom is the infringement of another's rights – but this is Amsterdam, so chill out!

To be fair to the authorities, over the last few years there has been a clean up in several areas, including dog faeces and hard drugs. The sex industry is generally well controlled and, as with drugs, it's unlikely to cause major offence unless you really going looking for the hard stuff.

A day in the life
of Amsterdam

It's 8.30am and the Centraal Station concourse feels a little like Peking. Only in China do more people take to the streets on two wheels, and the sheer density of cycle traffic makes this a very novel experience for most Europeans. The tram bells and bicycle bells ring their warning morning chorus, and heaven help you if you don't step out of their way.

Come night the squares of Leidseplein and Rembrandtplein, the streets of the Red Light District and a dozen other playgrounds of the Amsterdam night are brightly lit and humming with revellers. In the cold morning light they are hosed down and won't start waking again until midday or later. In fact the vampiric Red Light District won't rise again until cover of dark, though its hard-working hostesses will be back in their windows well before lunch.

The city's brown bars stir around 1100, offering a welcome coffee, and perhaps a slice of home-made apple cake. In the Grand Cafés, redolent of Belle Époque Paris, studious young men and women scramble for the newspapers on the reading desk. The Dutch are voracious media consumers, in both their mother tongue and English, and can be

disarmingly knowledgeable about the culture and history of their visitors' countries, particularly England. And it's not just the printed word they devour – for a fistful of small guilders they also surf the internet on street corner terminals.

The sleek glass-topped canal boats are now in full swing, almost queuing up to show their charges around the docks and grand canals. What is not apparent from this low-level viewing is Amsterdammers' love of window dressing, and showing off. The toothbrush shop window display is arranged as artfully as any of the city's multitude of galleries, and in grand canalside homes curtains are left ostentatiously open to flaunt oversized mirror-polished wooden furniture, bulging erudite bookcases and fulsome floral arrangements.

As the visitor's afternoon slips away browsing among Van Goghs and Rembrandts, in the cosy beery glow of a brown bar, or in the sweet smokey fug of a coffee shop where coffee is merely an excuse, the locals return from work to reclaim the streets, and their favourite bar stools.

For many Amsterdammers Thursday is the best day of all; the shops open late, new exhibitions and plays begin and there is an expectant buzz in the air.

A tram pulls off into the dusk with a lightning crackle above, its bell rings out and another Amsterdam night begins.

Yesterday and tomorrow

By the standards of many European capitals Amsterdam is a young city. In the late 13th century, when Paris was booming with a population of 100,000, Amsterdam was just emerging from its waterworld. A network of dams and dikes, ditches, sluices and windmills was built to tame, restrain and even harness the North Sea. The new city grew apace and within a few decades it had become one of northern Europe's leading ports.

Medieval times

During the Middle Ages Amsterdam prospered hugely from trade with England, Germany and the Baltic. Initially this was built on herrings and beer, though grain was to become its most important commodity. Trade was interrupted for most of the 16th century by the Spaniards who sought to Catholicise the burgeoning Netherlands. The Dutch Revolt ended both Spanish ambitions and also Catholicism in the Netherlands.

The Golden Age

Spain's north European campaign benefited Amsterdam when it seized the city's arch-rival, Antwerp. Not only was Amsterdam able to take its competitor's trade routes, but also many of its best people; Protestant refugees skilled in all manner of useful trades flooded into the city. Spain also proved inadvertently useful by driving Jewish refugees this way. Among many other skills, the Jews brought diamond expertise to Amsterdam. As the 16th century closed the Dutch discovered routes to the East Indies (Indonesia) and then set up the VOC or East India Company (*see pages 146–147*) to exploit their gains.

During the 17th century the city became a cosmopolitan melting-pot of traders famed for its interracial tolerance and trading prowess. Fabulous wealth poured into the city from all over the world; on the home front the arts flourished, producing such great painters as Rembrandt.

The city population was burgeoning rapidly and Amsterdam was taking on its present-day face, with the construction of the *Grachtengordel* (Canal Ring).

Decline

As the 17th century ended so Amsterdam's star was fading. The spirit of adventure was over, wars with England were sapping the country's strength and the VOC went bust. Amsterdam remained one of the world's financial capitals and the wealthiest city in Europe for many years but decadence set in and the country missed out on the Industrial Revolution.

The 20th century

Neutrality shielded the Netherlands from World War I, but not the horrors of World War II under the Nazi occupation,

most famously documented by Anne Frank (*see pages 80–81*).

In the 1960s Amsterdam was a hippy heaven, but it also saw an exciting period of social reform, spearheaded by the Provos (*see pages 42–43*) who paved the way for many of today's more socially and environmentally enlightened policies.

Amsterdam is now once more bidding to become a major international trade centre, particularly in the banking and telecommunication fields, and is renowned as a city of artists, architects, designers and publishers and experts in new media, such as the Internet.

People and places

Hardline socialist and former city mayor, Amsterdammer Ed van Thijn is the man who began policies to improve the city's image by stamping out squatters, hard drug traders and petty criminals. As a past government minister he was responsible for swingeing welfare budget cuts.

These days, with the help of his big business buddies, he is also literally changing the face of Amsterdam. Van Thijn was one of the main movers behind the highly controversial 'Stopera' development (*see page 120*) and is also involved in massive docklands redevelopments.

Mayor Schelto Patijn is another controversial establishment figure who has made himself unpopular by banning traditional street stalls on the eve of Koninginnedag (Queen's Day) and by introducing restrictions to this anarchic festival. He has also recently clamped down on dope-peddling coffee-shops and has banned the more explicit displays from sex-shop windows. However, many coffee-shop owners have applauded his measures, which at heart aim to separate out soft drugs and hard crime.

Football, films and monarchs

Ruud Gullit is one of the most gifted footballers ever to don the famous orange shirt of the Netherlands. The dapper dreadlocked one is based in the city, from where he shuttles to and from his job as manager of an English Premier League club, and also his fashion commitments in Milan.

These days, you're not likely to spot Queen Beatrix of the Netherlands on the streets of Amsterdam, but she did do a short stint in the Salvation Army in the Red Light District many years ago, and more recently, on Queen's Day, she went on an informal walkabout in the Jordaan, stopping to kiss a local, so it's said.

Holland's most famous film director, Paul Verhoeven, is living proof that sex and violence pays; *Basic Instinct*, *RoboCop*, *Total Recall* and the fleshy but critically panned *Showgirls* are all his work.

Margot Alvarez

Co-founder of *De Rode Draad* (the Prostitute's trade union) in 1988, Margot left after ten years' service to set up a new collective, which among other things will sort out the girls' accountancy problems and set up a prostitute's job agency. Although she must have had one of the hardest jobs in town she's the modest type, not to mention the master of the unintended pun, as a recent interviewer found out when asking about her future plans; 'it is a mistake to think that De Roode Draad will go flat on its back without me'.

Getting around

Bicycles

There is a cosy myth that Amsterdam is a cyclist's heaven. This is only partly true, if you are a local and know what you are doing. As a short-term visitor, don't even think about hiring a bicycle as a means of primary transport unless you are a skilled cyclist and well and truly acquainted with riding in a city environment. Even then you have to cope with riding on the right-hand side of the road, the intimidating presence of trams, a very large number of fellow cyclists plus conventional road traffic. And you must also remember that Amsterdam is notorious for bike theft. Lock your bike to an immovable object whenever you leave it, no matter how short a time you are away.

If you do venture out in the city on two wheels, wear a safety helmet, cover arms and legs in case of a spill, and check your insurance.

Taking a bicycle tour in the countryside is a completely different experience. Either go by yourself – Amsterdam Bos is a good option (*see page 150*) – or contact one of the city's several guided cycle tour operators through the VVV (the Dutch tourist office) (*see page 183*).

Car hire/driving in Amsterdam

This option is a complete no-no. If you arrive in a car find a safe place to park it (ask your hotel for the nearest location) and forget all about it for the duration of your stay.

Public transport

Trams

After walking, taking a tram is the best way of getting around. Trams serve all the destinations you will want to visit and run a very frequent service. Most (but not all) have a conductor at the back who will sell you a ticket. Just state your destination and the number in your party. If there is no conductor ask the driver. Transport staff speak good English.

In summer and at other popular holiday periods there is a special *Touristtram* service which passes all major attractions and enables you to hop on and off throughout the day for a flat fee.

Throughout the year the regular Circle-tram 20 service crosses the centre both ways, passing most major attractions and hotels.

Ticketing

You can buy an individual ticket each time you travel but this is expensive. If you are only spending a day in the city the inexpensive Day Ticket (*Dagkaart*) is the best buy. There are also Circle Amsterdam two-day and three-day passes, though the *strippenkaarten* (*see below*) system is probably a better bet.

You must buy a *strippenkaart* in advance, either from the GVB office (*see page 16*), a tobacconist or newsagent. It is a long bookmark-shaped ticket divided horizontally into 15 spaces numbered 1 to 15. Every time you ride you must fold your ticket back and insert it in the yellow ticket-stamping box on board the tram, to date and time stamp two of these spaces (ie so it stamps the second space down). You must add one space for each additional zone you go through: for example, on your first ride, presuming you stay within the same zone – which in most cases you will – stamp space No 2. If on your second trip you go outside the central area into a second zone, then you will use up three spaces so you will have to stamp space No 5, and so on.

Remember that your ticket, whether it is the valid portion on your *strippenkaart* or an individual ticket, is good for 1 hour on all public transport as long as you stay within the zone it is valid for. The same *strippenkaart* is also valid for public transport in other cities outside Amsterdam.

Buses

Buses cover some of the less popular routes that trams miss out. The driver will stamp your ticket.

Metro

Metro stops are positioned for Amsterdammers, not for tourists, and in general you won't be using the metro unless your hotel is adjacent to a metro stop. Ticketing machines are found at the metro entrance.

Night services

Trams and regular buses stop running at around midnight. Night buses (*nachtbusen*) then cover major routes at least every 30 minutes throughout the night.

It's tempting not to stamp your ticket or indeed not to bother with a ticket at all. Inspectors do occasionally board, however, and are strict in imposing a f60 on-the-spot fine if you don't have a ticket or if it has not been stamped. Being a tourist is no excuse.

General information

For information, tickets and maps on all public transport call at the GVB office (next to the VVV), opposite the Centraal Station main entrance.

Canal transport

Canal bus

This is a reasonable value hop-on, hop-off service with stops at the Rijksmuseum, Leidseplein. Keizersgracht / Raadhuisstraat, Westerkerk / Anne Frank House, Centraal Station and Stopera / Rembrandt House. There is a choice of two routes and it's a good idea if you're only here for a day or two.

For conventional canal boat tours (*see page 28*). A variation on this is the Museumboot, which departs every 30 minutes from Centraal Station, encircling the city and calling at the main museums.

Boats for hire

'Canal bikes' are pedalos which carry up to four persons. They are for hire at Stadhouderskade (by the Rijksmuseum), alongside Westerkerk, Leidsekade and the corner of Keizersgracht / Leidsestraat. Small motorboats are also for hire at various locations.

Taxis

Taxis are expensive and should only be used if there is no alternative. Hail one on the street, at a rank or ask your hotel to telephone for you. Tip 10 per cent.

Walking

This is by far the best way to get around the centre of town and in much of the Oude Zijde and Jordaan districts it is the only way, apart from cycling.

However, in the effort to make Amsterdam a cyclist's city it sometimes seems that pedestrians have been relegated to second-class citizens. There are three particular hazards: when crossing main roads many cyclists and motorcyclists regard traffic lights as optional; car drivers also disdain pedestrian lights; and when strolling by the canals you are fair game to any vehicle or cyclist if you are walking in between the phallic-shaped posts known as *Amsterdammer-chis*. You are supposed to walk on the outside of these although doing so renders you liable to falling in the canal, down basement stairs, and into tree roots, which often double as canine toilets. It's always wise to watch your step as you are gazing up at the canalside architecture roof tops.

An *Introduction to Amsterdam Walking Tour* leaves from the Victoria Hotel, opposite Centraal Station every Tue, Thur and Sat at 1000. Enquire at the VVV tourist office about this and other walking tours.

Don't miss

1 Amstelkring Museum

If you want to know how to 'hide' a church inside a house, step inside this amazing example of Amsterdammer's ingenuity and tolerance. **Page 49**

2 Anne Frankhuis

The famous story of suffering and heroism during Amsterdam's darkest days is told through the diary of a young teenage girl. **Pages 68–69**

3 Brown cafés

Chill out with a beer and some good food and discover the meaning of Dutch *gezelligheid*. **Page 174**

4 Canal cruise

This is the best way to see Amsterdam's grand canal architecture and is the perfect, easy introduction to the city. **Page 28**

5 Jordaan canals

The Jordaan's romantic leafy waterways, the antidote to Amsterdam's grand canals, are lived-in, chic, bohemian and just perfect for strolling. **Pages 66–75**

6 Kattenkabinet

You shouldn't leave the city without seeing inside at least one of its grand period canalside houses and, of the handful which do open their doors, this is the most entertaining. **Page 90**

7 Red-Light District

Love it or loathe it, you haven't seen Amsterdam until you've been here, preferably by night. **Pages 52-53**

8 Rijksmuseum

This fascinating museum is the treasure house of the nation not just the city, but pick your way through it carefully to avoid exhaustion. **Pages 92-97**

9 Scheepvartmuseum

Before Britannia ruled the waves Amsterdam was the hub of world maritime domination; come here and see how.
Page 138-139

10 Van Gogh Museum

This great display of easily accessible works by the world's most famous artist is complemented by lively captions, which move you briskly through his tragic life and exciting times. **Page 98-99**

Nieuwe Zijde

Centraal Station releases you into a heaving mass of commuters, fellow travellers, bicycles and trams. A huge barrel organ, hippy buskers and pleasure boats compete for your attention, much to the delight of pickpockets.

21

Getting there: All roads, tram lines, bus routes and train services lead to Centraal Station, and most canal bus services start and end at landing stages just outside the station.

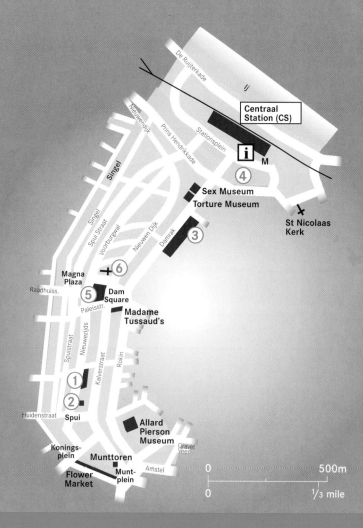

① Amsterdams Historisch Museum

The history of the city is displayed in easy manageable pieces at this fine museum. You can press the buttons and watch the growth of the city, compose your own carillon, and admire the huge pictures in the Civic Guard Gallery. **Page 24**

② Begijnhof

Begijnhof is a little bit of Amsterdam that's always at peace with itself. Save this historic close as a treat for when you're feeling stressed out and combine it with a visit to one or both of its two tiny churches. **Page 26**

③ Beurs van Berlage

This great square block may not look much from the outside but a tour inside is an unusual city highlight that will appeal to the architecturally inclined. A good place to escape the crowds, then look down on them, it's also an excellent concert venue.
Page 27

④ Canal cruise

You know you have to do it, so choose an operator with live commentary if possible then enjoy the passing parade of sublime canalside architecture. Sit at the back (outside) if you want to get the best pictures. **Page 28**

⑤ Koninklijk Paleis

It doesn't look much like a royal palace from inside or out, but the great marble reception hall is a truly memorable sight and the clearest sign of the confidence of the city during its Golden Age. **Page 30**

⑥ Nieuwe Kerk

Sadly you can only see inside the church when art exhibitions are on. These are often from the great treasure houses of the world, and the church makes a marvellous setting. **Page 32**

Tourist information

The city's main tourist information centre (VVV) (*see also page 183*) is opposite the station. It is open daily early until late and can book accommodation, tours and excursions, as well as being a mine of information (*tel: 0900 400 4040*). There is another, smaller but less busy office inside the station on platform 2.

Allard Pierson Museum

Allard Pierson Museum, Oude Turfmarkt 127 (off Rokin). Tel: 525 2556.
Tue–Fri 1000–1700, Sat–Sun 1300–1700. Tram 4, 9, 14, 16, 20, 24, 25. ££.

Behind the neo-classical façade of this grand 19th-century
building (once home to the Nederlandsche Bank) lies the
University of Amsterdam's collection of archaeological
artefacts. It comprises objects of art and everyday utensils,
mostly from ancient Egypt, Cyprus, Greece, Rome, Etruria,
Tuscany and the Near East, covering the period from
around 4000 BC to AD 1000. There are also plaster casts
of ancient Greek and Roman sculptures and models of the
pyramids and great temples.

Amsterdams Historisch Museum

Entrances on Kalverstraat 92, Sint Luciensteeg 27, Nieuwe Zijde Voorburgwal
357, Gedempte Begijnensloot, Begijnhof. Tel: 523 1822. Mon–Fri 1000–1700,
Sat–Sun 1100–1700. Tram 1, 2, 4, 5, 9, 14, 16, 20, 24, 25. ££.

The building that now houses the Amsterdam Historical
Museum was constructed in the late 16th century as the city
orphanage. Before you start exploring the history of the city
in the museum's main galleries, turn to your right. In the
first room a video gives a brief history of the building.
Look up to admire the strikingly beautiful painting *Orphan
Girls going to Church* (circa 1895), by Nicholas Van der
Waaij. Next to this room is the grand 17th-century Regent's
Chamber, where the orphanage's governors met, and finally
there is a room devoted to the orphanage's most famous
son, the naval hero Lieutenant Jan Van Speyk. He gained
immortality in 1831 when, declining to surrender his ship
to Belgian rebels in Antwerp, he blew up his attackers,
his ship and himself by dropping his cigar into a keg of
gunpowder. There wasn't much left of him but a piece of
his rib is on display here!

Chronology of the city

The first 17 rooms of the main exhibition area survey the chronology of the city, from its 13th-century origins up to the present day. The picture collection is particularly strong and the Golden Age is comprehensively covered. There are a few hands-on stations dotted throughout the museum, the best being in the loft, where you can compose your own tune on bells which came from the 17th-century carillon of the Munttoren (*see page 32*). It's also worth taking time to examine the exhibits on the Miracle of Amsterdam, particularly as this is a theme that may well recur elsewhere during your visit.

The Civic Guard Gallery

Fans of Rembrandt's famous painting *The Night Watch* (*see page 94*) can compare this masterpiece with the large-scale group portrait paintings of the same genre in the museum's Civic Guard Gallery. This unusual display is formed by a narrow alleyway running next to the museum, which has been glassed over and enclosed to become a picture gallery. Necessity was the mother of invention as the museum simply had no room elsewhere for these massive pictures. (In the orphanage's time this alleyway was an open sewer called Stink Ditch).

You don't have to pay the museum admission price to walk through the gallery but you won't be able to enjoy the high-level views which enable you to study the details of the pictures if you don't.

Begijnhof

Entrances at Spui 14 and via the Amsterdam Historisch Museum (Kalverstraat). Open from dawn, Kalverstraat gate closes 1700, Spui gate closes 2300. Roman Catholic Church Mon 1300–1800, Tue–Fri 0900–1830, Sat 0900–1700, Sun 0930–1700. English Church for services only. Tram 1, 2, 4, 5, 9, 14, 16, 20, 24, 25. Free.

The Beguines were a religious order of convent-dwelling women who devoted themselves to charitable work, without taking the usual vows of the nuns' sisterhood. The order was popular all over the Low Countries, and it made this close its Amsterdam home in 1346. However, the religious upheavals of 1578 meant that the Beguines, although still tolerated for their good works, had to worship in secret. Their clandestine Catholic church, built in 1671, is behind the façade of No 30, opposite the old convent church, subsequently renamed the Engelse Kerk (English Church) because it was rented to English (and Scottish) presbyterians.

Most of the homes around the courtyard were built in the 15th century but were altered throughout the 16th to 18th centuries. The notable exception is Het Outen Huis (the Wooden House) at No 34, which remains in its original state. This is the oldest house in Amsterdam, dating from around 1420.

The Beurs van Berlage (Be
in 1903, is proclaimed
20th-century buildin
comprising around 9
some 100m along th

The architect, Hend
the pioneer and pre
architecture. He wa
easily understood b
publico' – hence its
chambers, relieved a
and colourful tiles.

hall reopened in 1988 for
concerts and exhibitions,
and because of its fine
acoustics was adopted
by the Netherlands
Philharmonic Orchestra.
It has also recently opened
a permanent exhibition on
the building itself, which
allows you to get right
into its heart.

Highlights include the
medieval-style Berlage
Zaal, where the Chamber
of Commerce used to meet, and the capacious, galleried,
three-storey main exchange hall, with its superb glass-and-
wrought-iron roof. The 38m-tall tower is also open and gives
fine views over central Amsterdam.

There's only one real way to see Amsterdam and that's aboard a canal cruiser. These sleek, flat vessels are specially designed for navigating the city's low bridges and their curving windows and glass roofs allow maximum sightseeing visibility. There may be some variation but basically the major operators follow the same route: around the docks, then along the main waterways of the Amstel, Prinsengracht, Leidsegracht, Herengracht and Brouwersgracht. The trip takes around an hour.

Boats depart regularly from Prins Hendrikkade, opposite Centraal Station, and other places around the canals. As well as the regular tours the major operators offer brunch, dinner and candlelit cruises.

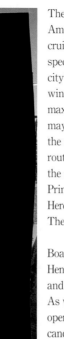

anal knowledge

*you are floating along on
ur canal cruise ponder this –
ll the canals and waterways
the city were laid end to end
y would stretch right across
Atlantic to New York, or
w Amsterdam as it was
wn when it was founded
the Dutch.*

Another option to consider is a Canal Cruise with the Canalbus company. You can hop on and off all day with stops at the Anne Frank House, Centraal Station, Rijksmuseum, Leidseplein, Westerkerk and the Stadhuis / Muziektheater. The fare is half as much again as the standard one-hour cruise but offers discounts off the admission price at various attractions. If you're intent on a day of serious cram-it-all-in sightseeing, particularly around the smaller museums, this might well be a good idea.

Centraal Station

Stationsplein 13. Tel: 069 292 or 0900 9292.

This great neo-Gothic, cathedral-like monument is probably Amsterdam's best-known landmark. Most visitors pass by here at least once, if not on arrival, then to catch a train (1400 pass through here every day) or bus, or take a boat cruise or visit the VVV tourist information office.

Centraal Station was built in 1889, designed partly by P J H Cuypers, who was also responsible for the Rijksmuseum, hence the similarity of the two buildings. Among the many details are sculptural references to the city's maritime trade and (on the left-hand side) its clock-style weather vane.

Dam Square

From Centraal Station the gaudy, heaving street of Damrak, chock-a-block with exchange bureaux and tacky souvenir

shops, leads to the Dam Square, Amsterdam's main square. As its name suggests, this was the site of the original dam which crossed the Amstel River and so put the dam in Amsterdam. There's no water to be seen today and the square is dominated by the Koninklijk Paleis (*see pages 30–31*), the Nieuwe Kerk (*see pages 32–33*) and Madame Tussaud's (*see page 31*). It's also peppered with second-rate buskers, fire-eaters, beggars and junkies, and is occasionally host to a fun fair.

By the Bijenkorf department store is the rather uninspired, ugly white National Monument, pledged to the dead of World War II and now a popular meeting-point. Its inscription means 'Never Again'. You probably won't want to linger too long here.

Koninklijk Paleis
(Royal Palace)

Dam Square. Tel: 620 4060. Daily June–July 1000–1800, daily Aug 1230–1700, Wed only Sept–May 1400–1600. Tour at 1400. Tram 1, 2, 4, 5, 9, 13, 14, 16, 17, 20, 24, 25. Bus 21. ££.

If Amsterdam's Royal Palace looks more like a municipal venue than the seat of kings then that's not surprising because this hulking great grey edifice was built in 1648 as the Stadhuis (town hall). Although its appearance is now gloomy and sooty, it was built as an expression of triumph in the era when Amsterdam was the world's most important trade centre and the 80-years war with Spain had just ended.

From its marble floor, where maps of the world are inlaid in the main chamber, up to its very pinnacle, where a golden ship sits on a weather vane, you will find symbols of the city's pre-eminent status. When it was built the Stadhuis was the biggest town hall in Europe, and the 17th-century poet Huygens was moved to describe it as 'The Eighth Wonder of the World'.

The Stadhuis acquired its royal nomenclature in less happy times for the country when, in 1808, the French invaded. Louis Napoleon (brother of Napoleon Bonaparte) declared himself King of the Netherlands and moved his court here.

The focus of the palace is the Burgerzaal (Citizens' Hall), a magnificent, echoing marble chamber that based on the assembly halls of ancient Rome runs for some 30m along the whole length of the building. Six huge crystal chandeliers above and three great maps of the world set in the marble below draw the eye.

The functions of the various rooms and areas around the Burgerzaal may be deduced from their sculptures and paintings: in the Tribunal (an area used only for pronouncing the death sentence) the Greek legislator Zaleucus permits one of his own eyes to be burned out in order to save his son from total blindness; above the Bankruptcy Office Icarus falls after flying too close to the sun; more happily, Venus is found above the room where marriages were registered. The furniture is of the ponderous Empire style, introduced by the conquering French.

A decade after Napoleon, King William I returned the building to the city government, but it retained its name and royal status and is still used today for occasional royal functions.

Madame Tussaud's Scenarama

Dam 20. Tel: 622 9949. Daily 1000–1730, July–Aug 0930–1930. Tram 1, 2, 4, 5, 9, 13, 14, 16, 17, 20, 24, 25. Bus 21. £££.

Want to come face-to-face with Rembrandt, walk through a Vermeer or Steen painting, listen to William of Orange and learn a little (but certainly no more than a little) about Amsterdam's Golden Age? Then roll up, roll up to Madame T's. Among the celebrities there are Princess Diana, Arnold Schwarzeneger, Oprah Winfrey and Tina Turner.

Magna Plaza (Postkantoor)

Nieuwezijds Voorburgwal (off Dam Square). Daily. Tram 1, 2, 4, 5, 9, 13, 14, 16, 17, 20, 24, 25. Bus 21.

Since 1990 the Magna Plaza shopping centre has been the new incarnation of the old Postkantoor (main post office building). Originally built in 1899, its grand exterior is topped by three handsome spires while inside its five floors are set around a huge atrium surrounded by beautiful, arcaded brick galleries.

It was ridiculed in its time as 'post-office Gothic' and certainly looks as if it should have housed something far more important than a post office. Whether or not you intend shopping in this neo-Gothic mall, it's well worth a look. (*See page 39*).

Munttoren (Mint Tower)

Muntplein. Tram 1, 2, 5 to Koningsplein, 4, 9, 14, 16, 24, 25 to Muntplein.

This handsome tower marks the confluence of the Singel and the Amstel rivers and is a city landmark. Its brick base was once the Regulierspoort, a gate in the old city walls, built around 1490. After fire destroyed the top half of the tower the present clock tower was added in 1619 and during the late 17th century it was briefly used as a mint, hence its name. Today it is home to a gift shop (*see page 40*). A carillon rings out every 15 minutes.

On the other side of the Singel is the Bloemenmarkt, Amsterdam's main flower market (*see page 40*).

Nieuwe Kerk (New Church)

Dam. Tel: 638 6900 (recorded information). Opening hours and admission price dependent upon exhibitions and events. Tram 1, 2, 4, 5, 9, 13, 14, 16, 17, 20, 24, 25. Bus 21.

The Nieuwe Kerk is only 'new' in relation to the Oude Kerk (Old Church, *see page 51*), as its construction began in the late 14th century. It was appreciably enlarged and added to over the next two-and-a-half centuries, but Calvinists stripped it of its altars and statues in 1578, and disaster struck in 1645 when it was gutted by fire.

Today the church is largely bare, but among its few remaining outstanding monuments and furnishings are

some splendid pieces from the Golden Age. The principal highlights are the magnificent painted Great Organ and huge ornately carved pulpit resembling a small pagoda.

*n it's Spring again
*ring again tulips
* Amsterdam' goes
*ld song. Tulips are
available all year
*d, and you can buy
*s in bloom or tulip
*s by the sackload
* the Bloemenmarkt,
*he Netherlands'
est flower export is
ally roses.*

Look out too for its splendid wooden ceiling, the bronze choir screen and the tomb of Admiral Michiel de Ruyter (1607-76), one of many Dutch naval heroes entombed here. The country's greatest poet, Vondel, is commemorated here too, by a small urn near the entrance.

River IJ

Behind the station is the River IJ (pronounced *ey* as in they) and the sea, though the station building has so effectively blocked this out that you could almost forget that Amsterdam is a port. It's worth having a look here to see the ferries chugging to and fro and to compare this workaday scene to the frenetic activity at the front of the building.

On Sundays (Apr–mid Oct) an historic ferry departs from De Ruyterkade landing No 8 at 1200, 1400 and 1600 for a tour around the northern docks.

Sex Museum Venus Tempel

Damrak 18. Daily 1000–2300. Tram 4, 9, 16, 20, 24, 25. £.

The museum examines the depiction of sex through the ages, with, for example, hard-core ancient Indian and Far Eastern sculptures proving that the Dutch did not invent sex. Early videos of the days when a glimpse of stocking was, quite literally, looked upon as something shocking, are genuinely amusing, and this museum has plenty of other lighter moments too. Predictably the most popular area is the one which warns of the most explicit and sensational material, though at least the participants appear to be consenting adults.

It's good value for the admission price, but don't take your maiden aunt.

Singel

Singel means 'moat' and the northern stretch of this major canal holds a number of curiosities. The landmark dome belongs to the Luthersekerk (Lutheran Church), built in 1670 and attributed to the city's famous architect, Hendrick de Keyser.

On the Kattengat side of the church are two very picturesque houses, dating from 1614, with the bewitching names of De Gouden Spiegel (The Golden Mirror) and De Silveren Spiegel (The Silver Mirror). The latter now houses one of the city's best restaurants (*see page 38*).

Back on the canal path look for No 7 Singel. Tour guides delight in pointing this out as the narrowest house in Amsterdam – though it is only the very front of the house which is so narrow; behind it broadens out to more conventional dimensions.

Moored close by outside No 40 is the Poezenboot ('Pussy Boat'), a refuge for around 150 stray cats. It is open to visitors (*daily 1300–1500*). Continue south along the canal and you will see a number of window girls. This marks a small Red-Light district just behind the Singel on and around Oude Nieuwstraat.

At the next bridge, the very wide Torensteeg (also called the Torensluis), look in the bridge foundations for what was once a 17th-century prison. The poor unfortunates locked in here would find themselves waist deep in water as the tides washed in and out of the canal.

Spui/Spuistraat

Getting there: Tram 1, 2, 4, 5, 9, 14, 16, 20, 24, 25.

The name of this small tree-lined square means 'sluice' and is pronounced (roughly) *Schpow* – listen to the tram drivers for the real vernacular. It is famous for its horribly twee statue of a boy known as *Het'Lieverdje*, loosely translated as 'The Little Urchin' or 'Little Darling'. It was donated by a tobacco company in the 1960s and became a rallying point for Amsterdam's Provos movement (*see pages 42–43*).

A far cry from the revolutionary ideals of the 1960s is the large number of fashionable eating and drinking options around Spui, many of which occupy handsome 17th-century buildings at the southern end of Spuistraat.

Narrow houses

The reason why No 7 Singel is so narrow and why, in general, Amsterdam's canalside houses go back and upwards rather than across, is that tax was levied according to the width of the house.

Just across the Singel is the landmark twin-towered Krijtberg Church. A couple of doors away is the Odeon, a handsome canalside house, built by the acclaimed architect Philips Vingboons in 1622. A concert room was added to the first floor in 1837, apparently acoustically designed in a parabolic shape to the calculations of a mathematician. You can test it out yourself most nights as the Odeon is now a throbbing nightclub (*see page 41*).

Torture Museum

20–22 Damrak. Tel: 639 2027. Daily 1000–2300. Tram 4, 9, 16, 20, 24, 25. ££.

The Torture Museum is an unpleasant trawl through dark Dutch deeds and European medieval horrors. Gasp at the guillotine, squirm at the Inquisition Chair, cross your legs at some of the unmentionable goings-on and ask yourself, 'Why on earth did I come in here in the first place?' Definitely for the macabre-minded only.

Cafés

Smits Koffiehuis

Stationsplein 10. Tel: 623 3777. Most people rush past this café, tucked below the VVV tourist office in their effort to get away from the station. It's almost completely divorced from the hubbub, however, with a floating terrace and a pleasant dining area for full meals. *Daily 1000–2100.*

David and Goliath

Kalverstraat 92. Tel: 622 6736. You don't need to visit the Amsterdam Historisch Museum (*see pages 24–25*) to use its attractive barn-like café, which was once the orphanage cowshed. Gazing down upon you is the extraordinary two-storey-high wooden statue of Goliath, which once graced an Amsterdam pleasure park. Good varied menu of snacks and full meals. *Mon–Fri 1000–1700, Sat–Sun 1100–1700.*

OIBIBIO

Prins Hendrikkade 20–21. Tel: 553 9355. Its strange name means the 'Art of Being' and it opened in 1994 as an alternative lifestyle centre incorporating a Grand Café, vegetarian restaurant, Japanese tea garden, shop (*see page 39*), sauna and other New Age activities good for body and soul. The beautiful designer art deco-style grand café is one of the finest in Amsterdam. Its eastern-inspired meals may get mixed reviews, but its oriental tea garden (shoes off, please) with waterfall and fishes is pure joy. Just the place to unwind after the mayhem of Centraal Station across the road. *Grand Café daily 0900–late; restaurant 1730–2200; tea garden 1000–1900.*

Greenwoods

Singel 103. Tel: 624 9382. This small, hole-in-the-wall café specialises in teas, home-made cakes, all-day breakfasts, quiches, bagels and muffins. Friendly, homely atmosphere. *Mon–Fri 0930–1900, Sat–Sun 1100–1900.*

1e Klas

Platform 2b, Centraal Station. Tel: 625 0131. ££. The name alludes to the former function of this art deco-styled café-restaurant as the first-class passengers' waiting room. Perfect for a brief encounter between railway romantics. *Daily 0930–2300.*

Café Luxembourg

Spui 24. Tel: 620 6264. The terrace of this Grand Café is one of the area's prime spots for people-watching, but expect to pay over the odds for the privilege. Popular with a trendy crowd; packed to the gills on live music nights. *Daily 1000–late.*

Bars

Drie Fleschjes

Gravenstraat 16 (behind the Nieuwe Kerk). This atmospheric old bar (its name means The Three Bottles) dates from 1650. There's usually standing room only. Note its collection of liqueur bottles, on which are painted the portrait of every mayor of Amsterdam since 1591. *Mon–Sat 1200–2015, Sun 1500–1900.*

Hoppe

Spuistraat 18–20. One of Amsterdam's best-known watering holes and former favourite of brewing magnate Freddy Heineken, this earthy, small, old-fashioned sand-strewn bar has been serving beer and liqueurs since 1670. In summer the crowds spill out on to the pavement and it is difficult to get near the bar. *Daily 0800–0100/0200.*

Wijnand Fockink

Pijlsteeg 31 (off Dam Square, behind Hotel Krasnapolsky). Established in 1679, Wijnand Fockink's collection of jars and bottles might make you think you had wandered into a tiny museum or an ancient apothecary's shop. Indulge yourself by trying one of its many fruit-flavoured *jenevers* (gins). *Daily 1500–2100.*

De Wildeman

Nieuwezijds Kolk 5. Beer drinkers are spoiled for choice at this atmospheric bar, founded in 1690, with some 18 types on draught and around 200 bottled. The barstaff are very helpful and there is the unusual luxury of a non-smoking room. *Mon–Fri 1200–0100/0200, Sat 1400–2100.*

Restaurants

Dorrius

Nieuwezijdsvoorburgwal 5. Tel: 420 2224. ££. This lovely old house serves traditional Dutch food with a French twist. Try Zeeland oysters in season or the famous 'Dorrius cheese soufflé'. Large portions. *Daily 1730–2300.*

Haesje Claes

Spuistraat 273–5. Tel: 624 9998. ££–£££. A charming, quintessentially old-time Dutch restaurant with bags of atmosphere and an exclusively Dutch menu which specialises in hotpots and fish stews. Try their eel and salmon with lobster. *Daily 1200–2200.*

Kantijl & de Tijger

Spuistraat 291–3. Tel: 620 0994. ££. Good-value, authentic Indonesian cooking in a modern, rather bright and often very busy dining-room. *Daily 1700–2300.*

Keuken van 1870

Spuistraat 4. Tel: 624 8965. £. It resembles a school dining-room and you'll probably be the only non-local in here, but ask the friendly 'dinner ladies' what they recommend from the all-Dutch menu and it's hard to go wrong. *Mon–Fri 1230–2000, Sat–Sun 1600–2100.*

Lucius

Spuistraat 247. Tel: 624 1831. ££. If you're serious about fish and you prize the quality of the food above the atmosphere then go along to the white-tiled dining-room of Lucius and choose the catch of the day from their blackboard. *Mon–Sat 1700–2400.*

Oud Holland

Nieuwezijdsvoorburgwal 105. Tel: 624 6848. £–££. Traditional Dutch food is served in this simple eating-house set in a 17th-century building with a front terrace. *Daily 1200–2130.*

Port Van Cleve

Nieuwezijdsvoorburgwal 178–80. Tel: 624 0047. ££–£££. This handsome Amsterdam landmark offers a choice of two spacious restaurants where you can sample classic traditional Dutch cuisine or one of the hotel's famous steaks. Each is individually numbered and to date they have served over six million. Have an aperitif in the hotel's De Blaue Parade, surrounded by blue Delft tiles. *Daily 0700–2230.*

De Roode Leeuw

Damrak 93–4. Tel: 555 0666. ££–£££. By day the Roode Leeuw's front terrace is crowded with tourists curious to sample real Dutch cooking. In the evening this closes and the atmosphere and prices move up-market and inside to the more formal dining-room. *Daily noon–2130.*

De Silveren Spiegel

Kattengat 4. Tel: 624 6589. £££. Occupying one of the city's most picturesque 17th-century houses, the Silver Mirror is acclaimed for its fine Dutch cuisine and is famous for its lamb, which comes from the North Sea island of Texel. *Mon–Fri 1200–1400, 1800–2200; Sat 1800–2200.*

Treasure

Nieuwezijdsvoorburgwal 115. Tel: 623 4061. £££. Generally regarded as the best Chinese restaurant in Amsterdam, with specialist Cantonese, Peking, Szechuan and Shanghai chefs offering authentic regional tastes. Renowned, too, for its lunchtime *dim sum* with over 50 types usually on offer. *Daily 1200–1500, 1700–2230.*

Vijff Vliegen

Spuistraat 294–302. Tel: 624 8369. £££. The Five Flies may be an inauspicious name for a restaurant, but there's not a more romantic, cosy, traditional eating house in Amsterdam than this one. It is spread over five 17th-century houses packed with antiques, and one room even features etchings by Rembrandt. The cooking is a mix of Dutch and French styles and generally pleases but is accused of being overpriced. *Daily 1730–2200.*

Shopping

Kalverstraat is the city's main shopping thoroughfare. It's all pedestrianised and tends towards an international style of anonymity, but if you can stand wading through the tat and jostling with the crowds then there are some reasonable places to be found. Quality improves the further south you go, with many of its best shops now located in the new Kalvertoren centre (see below).

Department stores/malls

De Bijenkorf

Dam Square. Amsterdammers swarm to the Beehive department store. It's known for its household goods and particularly its clothing, as illustrated by the imaginative, often striking, window displays.

Kalvertoren

Kalverstraat, also entrance off Heiligeweg. Oilily, H&M, Mango Boss, Hema, DKNY and Leonidas are familiar names at this smart new centre, which includes three levels of shops and a sixth-floor café with panoramic views. The Café Marché inside Vroom & Dreesman bookshop is also recommended. *Daily.*

Magna Plaza

Nieuwezijds Voorburgwal (off Dam Square). Amsterdam's first and finest mall and a pioneer of seven-day shopping. The building (*see page 31*) is one of the city's architectural triumphs and the 40 shops provide good browsing for a rainy day; options include a touristy cheese stand, top-class wooden toys, Virgin Megastore, several expensive high-quality fashionwear outlets and a pair of trendy cafés. *Daily.*

Maison de Bonneterie

Rokin 140–2. This small, old-fashioned, 100-year-old, up-market department store grandly claims to be the most beautiful in the Netherlands and has earned the seal of approval of Queen Beatrix. It is worth a look just for its sweeping balustrades and glass cupola. High-quality designer clothing, household goods and soft furnishings are its stock-in-trade. *Daily.*

OIBIBIO/Warenhuis

Prins Hendrikkade 20–21. Located below the OIBIBIO Grand Café (*see page 36*) this shop continues the New Age theme with music, books and all sorts of ethnic and esoteric items whose stated objective is to make spirituality and conciousness-raising available to a wider public. It makes fascinating browsing. There's an excellent household goods and gifts department upstairs (including cosmetics and paperware). *Daily.*

Specialists

Amsterdam Diamond Centre

Rokin 1. A member of the Amsterdam Diamond Foundation, open for tours (*see page 87*).

Athaeneum Boekhandel & Nieuwscentrum

Spui 14–16. This fine old art nouveau-style shop is a favourite browsing place (particularly for non-fiction titles) for students and Spui's trendy café crowds.

Bloemenmarkt (Flower Market)

Singel, between Muntplein and Koningsplein. The Bloemenmarkt is a tourist attraction in its own right – though it is certainly not all it's cracked up to be and you can hardly tell the famous floating stalls are afloat at all. It comprises around 15 florists and garden shops on permanently moored barges and is popular with locals as well as tourists. There are many exotic varieties available, as well as the usual tulips, roses and carnations. *Daily.*

PGC Hagenius

Rokin 92–6. Hagenius has the refined atmosphere of a gentlemen's club and is a shrine to tobacco. Choose from the best selection of cigars in town and browse the museum-quality displays of pipes and smoking paraphernalia. The lovely shop interior dates from the 1920s. *Daily.*

Holland Gallery de Munt

Munttoren, Muntplein. Royal Delft and Makkum ware are the main attractions at this small high-class gift store ensconced in one of the city's historic landmarks (*see page 32*).

H P De Vreng En Zonen

Nieuwendijk 75. This beautiful distillers-cum-wine and spirit shop is totally out of place on scruffy Nieuwendijk. It distils its own *jenevers* (gins) and its exquisite presentation bottles of all kinds of Dutch drinks make a perfect present. It also boasts the world's largest collection of miniatures, verified at over 15,000 by the Guinness Book of Records.

De Klompenboer (The Clog Factory)

Nieuwezijdsvoorburgwal 20 (also rear entrance on Spuistraat). Amsterdam's favourite *klompen* shop proves that not all wooden shoes have to be decorated with windmills and stuck on the mantelpiece (though it sells plenty of these too). Clogs are made on the premises, so if you don't like what you see on the racks, a bespoke pair can be quickly carved for you.

Nightlife

Odeon

Singel 460. There's a floor for every taste here – head to the top for 1970s disco fever, get down to ground for house and jazz dance. *Nightly 2200–0400/0500.*

RoXY

Singel 465. Famed as the club with the choosiest door policy in town, the RoXY attracts the country's top DJs and is said to have the city's best sound system playing mostly house music. Wed–Sun 2300–0400/0500.

Provos and Gnomes

Amsterdam's present reputation for humanist, creative and liberal free-thinking politics has much to do with the events of the 1960s and the movement known as the Provos.

The Provos (whose name simply means 'to provoke') were initially a group of anarchic individuals who protested against much of the status quo of this era, specifically against consumerism and most notably against tobacco. What brought them fame and attention was the bizarre style of both their protests and their leaders: Robert Jasper Grootveld, the 'anti-smoke sorceror', danced in body paint,

smoked to take on the sins of the world and chanted a weird smoker's cough; the acrobatic poet, Johnny (the Self Kicker) van Doom, was a reciter of incessant mantras; and Bart Hughes trepanned himself (drilled a hole in his head) to give himself 'a third eye' in order to raise his level of conciousness. These were no ordinary politicos!

The statue of Het'Lieverdje on Spui became a focal point for the Provos' 'happenings'; anarchic protests which nowadays would simply be laughed off. But their goals were serious and in the climate of the 1960s they were seen as a threat to the establishment. The police response was often unnecessarily heavy-handed. The Provos began to make friends in the

mainstream and issues such as drugs, homelessness and the environment were given a serious platform.

The Provos' most famous suggestion was the provision of free white bicycles for everyone. The police impounded the first white bicycle but a small number were made available for public use. Within a few days all were stolen!

The Provos disbanded in 1967 but their torch was carried by the Kabouters (Gnomes), who combined the Provos' free spirits and broad philosophy with a more realistic and worldly approach. In the 1970 elections they won 11 per cent of the vote, though today they have all but gone from the political scene.

Oude Zijde

The old part of town is dominated by the image, if not the reality, of the Red-Light District. There's plenty more to see than a few window girls, and once you reach the boundary of this tightly confined district the change in appearance and atmosphere is striking. The influence of both the University and the docks is also very important in this most colourful of city areas.

BEST OF

Oude Zijde

Getting there: The Oude Zijde is just a few minutes' walk from Centraal Station. Trams and buses don't penetrate into the narrow streets and canals around the Red-Light District and University, so walking is the only way of exploring much of this area.

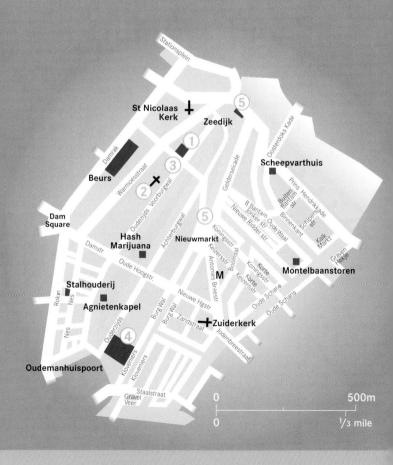

① Amstelkring Museum

This remarkable secret church demonstrates not only the lengths that the persecuted were prepared to go to in the 17th century, but also the deceptive size of an Amsterdam canal house. **Page 49**

② Oude Kerk

The dark, cavernous, brooding ancient church is an atmospheric place and as memorable for its juxtaposition cheek-by-jowl with the city's prostitutes as any architectural highlights. **Page 51**

③ Red-Light District

Take a walk on the wild side by night to see the Red-Light District at its most extreme. Keep to the main thoroughfares and you should be perfectly safe. **Page 52**

④ University area

If your soul has taken a battering from the sleaze of the Red-Light District it's comforting to walk just a few yards to the handsome buildings, buzzing cafés and bright young things of Amsterdam's main University area. **Page 55**

⑤ De Waag and Schreierstoren

Two of Amsterdam's oldest buildings, each now converted into atmospheric cafés, have more than a few tales to tell. Visit the Waag by night, when it is lit by candles. **Page 50** (De Waag); **Page 54** (Schreierstoren)

47

Hash Marijuana
(Hemp Museum)

Oudezijds Achterburgwal 148. Daily 1100–2200. Tram 4, 9, 14, 16, 24, 25. ££.

With many countries now debating the rights and wrongs of legalising cannabis this might be a good place to get clued up on the benefits of smoking dope. Just as candid depictions of sexual behaviour were copied by the Dutch from the early Asiatic cultures of their empire, so too the smoking of hemp first caught on in 1554, under oriental influence. Originally it was seen as a cure for earache – though we doubt that you would get away with that excuse today.

Montelbaanstoren

Oude Schans 2. Tram 9, 14 to Nieuwmarkt.

The lower brick part of this tower was built in 1512 as part of the city's fortifications and the wooden superstructure was added at the beginning of the 17th century. Unfortunately the meaning of its name is lost in the mists of time.

> " *The women are not particularly engaging. One sees few slim waists, they do have pale complexions, but are devoid of personality. Excessive coffee and tea-drinking ruins their teeth completely.* "
>
> **Marquis de Sade, 1769**

As this was the last glimpse of Amsterdam that sailors of the East India Company had before being ferried to their ships to make their long and hazardous voyages, the Montelbaanstoren became a popular romantic subject for artists. You will probably spot it in the Rijksmuseum, in etchings by Rembrandt, and other galleries. These days it has a more prosaic function, home to municipal offices, and is not open to the public.

Museum Amstelkring
(Ons' Lieve Heer op Solder)

Oudezijds Voorburgwal 40. Tel: 624 6604. Mon–Sat 1000–1700,
Sun 1300–1700. Tram 4, 9, 16, 24, 25. ££.

As a result of the Dutch Reformation of 1578 ('the Alteration'),
when Amsterdam shifted from being Catholic to Protestant,
Catholics were forbidden to practise their religion in public.
Consequently a number of fully furnished *schuilkerken*
(clandestine churches) began to spring up in private homes.
They were not recognisable as churches from the outside
and had to run along the side of the house as opposed to
the front; likewise the church entrance had to be from the
side alley.

Ons' Lieve Heer op Solder (Our Lord in the Attic) is not
the only hidden church left in the city, but it is the only
17th-century survivor of this tradition in its original state
and open to the public.

In fact it is actually three houses in one. The first house,
through which you enter, was built between 1661 and 1663
for hosiery merchant Jan Hartmann. On the ground floor
was a shop with an office behind. The domestic highlight
is the adjacent Sael, the reception room, in heavy Dutch
classicist style. It's on and upwards to explore the church
and its chapel, then various other rooms before finally
descending to a fully equipped 19th-century kitchen, a
library, and back to the front door.

Nieuwmarkt

Getting there: Tram 9, 14.

Nowadays Nieuwmarkt (New Market) stands rather forlorn, a broad, empty space host to a small general market through the week, a farmers' market on Saturdays and an antiques and curios market from May through September. Yet this was once a teeming space full of Amsterdammers doing their daily shopping and boats came right into the square along the Geldersekade.

Dominating the space is De Waag (The Weighhouse), resembling a miniature medieval fortress. It was built in 1488 as a gate in the city wall and takes its name from its 17th-century function as public weighhouse. Prior to this, Nieuwmarkt was an execution site and condemned prisoners spent some of their last hours in the Waag. Later in the century trade guilds used the upper rooms as a meeting place.

The octagonal tower in the centre of the building was added in 1690–1 and used as the Theatricum Anatomicum, the lecture theatre of the Surgeons' Guild. It was made famous in various paintings by Rembrandt, the prime example being *The Anatomy Lesson of Dr Tulp*. Today the only flesh being sliced is in the kitchen of the trendy café-restaurant that now occupies the building (*see page 58*).

> " The whores were still there. They sat in luminous body stockings in windows lit with a pinkish glow, and winked at me as I passed. ("Hey, they like me!" I thought, until I realised that they do this for everybody.) Behind them I could glimpse the little cells where they conduct their business, looking white and clinical, like some place you would go to have your haemorrhoids seen to. "

Bill Bryson, *Neither Here Nor There*, 1991

Oude Kerk (Old Church)

Oudekerksplein. Tel: 625 8284. Mon–Sat 1100–1700, Sun 1300–1700. Tower June–Sept 1400–1600. Tram 4, 9, 14, 16, 24, 25. £.

As its name suggests, this is a place of great antiquity – indeed it is the city's oldest church, founded in the early 13th century, though the present building dates largely from the 14th and 15th centuries. It is quite difficult to appreciate just what an impressive Gothic structure the Oude Kerk is, as it is hemmed in by buildings from every side. This is also the heart of the Red-Light District and as you walk around the church, north from the main entrance, you are met face on by a terrace of window girls who look straight on to one side of the Oude Kerk. It certainly makes it difficult to concentrate on studying ecclesiastical architecture.

The main points of interest are its great organ, added in 1724, the gilded 15th-century ceiling (difficult to make out in the gloom) and the Lady Chapel, with a fine stained-glass window (1552) that was restored after the Alteration.

The church is dedicated to St Nicholas, the patron saint of sailors, and the maritime connection is evident by ship models and the tombs of Admirals van der Hulst and van Heemskerk. Look, too, for the plain slab simply marked 'Saskia', which marks the grave of Rembrandt's wife.

The tower is open in summer and gives a fine view of the Oude Zijde part of town. On Saturdays, between 1600 and 1700, a carillon is rung on the church's 17th-century bells.

Oudemanhuispoort

Entrances on Oudezijds Achterburgwal and Kloveniersburgwal. Tram 4, 9, 14, 16, 24, 25.

The name of this arched brick passageway means 'the gate to the old man's home', referring to the almshouses which were built here in 1754. These buildings were taken over by the university in 1879 and are not open to the public, though you can step inside to admire their lovely courtyard from a door halfway along the passage. Much better known is the book market which is held in the passage from Monday to Saturday.

Red-Light District

For better or for worse Amsterdam's Red-Light District is now an established port-of-call on most tourists' itineraries, ranking alongside, if not above, the Anne Frank House and the Rijksmuseum. In fact, most of the people you will see wandering the street are fellow visitors and by strength of numbers alone there is little to fear here in terms of personal security, as long as you stick to the main streets and shun the advances of the shady drugs dealers and pimps.

The other thing that you should never do in the Red-Light District is attempt to take pictures of the girls. Leave your camera at the hotel.

It's perfectly safe to visit the sex shops (the vast majority of which are legitimate businesses), and in theory you should not be ripped off by the live sex shows either, though use your discretion about paying large sums of money to spivvy-looking characters leading you into dark alleyways.

The best bet for raunchy theatre in Amsterdam, without fear of being ripped off, is either the Bananenbar or the Casa Rosso, both of which are well established, used to dealing with tourists and are the most respectable – or least seedy – of their ilk (*see page 61*).

Red-Light tours

Those fun-loving folk at Boom Chicago (*see page 104*) offer two-hour guided walking tours of the Red-Light District which take a look at the history and architecture of this part of town ... plus a peek at the windows. *Tours leave the Leidseplein Theater at 1600. Tel: 530 7309.* See also Amsterdam's Sex Trade (*pages 62–63*).

St Nicolaas Kerk

Prins Hendrikkade (opposite Centraal Station). Tram 1, 2, 4, 5, 9, 11, 13, 16, 17, 24, 25.

Looks flatter to deceive at this grandiose harbourside church. It was built in 1887 in neo-baroque style by the congregation of Ons' Lieve Heer op Solder (Our Lord in the Attic, *see page 49*) when the ban on Catholic worship was raised. However, it is quite plain inside, has rarely been used this century and at present is hidden under scaffolding and sheets of tarpaulin, undergoing restoration. The church is only open to the public for classical music concerts, usually held on Sundays at 1700.

Scheepvarthuis

Prins Hendrikkade 108. Tel: 625 8908. Tram 1, 2, 4, 5, 9, 11, 13, 16, 17, 24, 25.

Not to be confused with the Scheepvart Museum (Maritime Museum, *see pages 138–139*), the striking Shipping House, built in 1916, is regarded as the first example of the renowned Amsterdam School of architecture, which in this particular case foreshadows art deco with its exuberant stone carvings. It is now used for municipal offices and is only open to the public by guided tours, booked in advance.

Schreierstoren

Prins Hendrikkade. Tram 1, 2, 4, 5, 9, 11, 13, 16, 17, 24, 25.

Another structure which formed part of Amsterdam's original fortified medieval city walls, the Schreierstoren has more than a passing resemblance to a giant orange squeezer. It's name romantically translates to the 'Weeping Tower' or 'Tower of Tears', and this is one of the points where women used to bid farewell to their seagoing menfolk. A more prosaic explanation is that the tower lies on a sharp bend (*screye*) and this is the reason for its name.

Whatever, there is no doubt that Henry Hudson set sail from here in 1609 to discover a quicker trading route to the East Indies. Like Columbus, he blundered into the Americas and by serendipity was immortalised by the Hudson River and Hudson Bay.

The tower is now occupied by the VOC café-restaurant, which has returned a couple of its rooms to its Golden Age appearance (*see page 59*).

Universiteit van Amsterdam

The University of Amsterdam was only founded in 1877 but its roots go back centuries and its heart is still very much here in the southernmost part of the Oudezijds, enclosed by the Amstel, Grimburgwal, Kloveniersburgwal and Slijkstraat. Though most of its buildings are not open to the public, you can visit the Agnietenkapel (St Agnes Chapel) at Oudezijds Voorburgwal 231 (*open Mon–Fri 0900–1700*) to see an introductory video on the early history of the university. Close by, at the confluence of the Oudezijds Voorburgwal and the Oudezijds Achterburgwal, is the **Huis aan de Drie Grachten** (House on the Three Canals), built in 1609 with three splendid step-gabled façades, each looking on to a different canal.

Warmoesstraat

This was one of Amsterdam's very first streets and for centuries was a prestigious address and principal shopping thoroughfare. Mozart and Marx came here in its halcyon days but today Warmoesstraat is the defining western boundary of the Red-Light District and has become almost a by-word for sleaze.

Beside the porno shops, coffee shops and seedy clubs, however, are some worthwhile eating places and at its southern end two contrasting shops which sum up Amsterdam's schizophrenic, laid-back character. The first, which belongs to a much more genteel age, is **Geel's and Co Thee en Koffiehandel**, an old-fashioned tea-and-coffee merchant. Downstairs in the main shop area are various delicious, heady aromas, while upstairs is an array of vintage blenders, roasters, grinders, percolators and other coffee paraphernalia, which the staff happily demonstrate to anyone showing interest.

Adjacent is one of Amsterdam's most famous specialist shops, **Condomerie Het Gulden Vlies** (The Golden Fleece Condom Shop), where you can buy prophylactics of all sizes, shapes, textures, colours (some are hand-painted!) and even flavours, all nicely gift-wrapped. Strangely, given its nature and location, it's all done in surprisingly good taste.

If neither coffee - nor chocolate-flavoured condoms are to your taste, go next door to **De Tulp** (The Tulip), yet another example of the city's penchant for retail specialism.

Zeedijk

Zeedijk was one of Amsterdam's original fortifications, built in the early 1300s, and at No 1 is one of only two wooden houses surviving in the city (the other is in the Begijnhof, *see page 26*). It is now occupied by the Café In't Aepjen (*see page 58*). Opposite is St Olafskapel with a similar medieval pedigree.

Zeedijk has long had a bad reputation, stretching back to the 17th century when the East India Company sailors used to come here for their rest and relaxation. During the 1960s and 1970s it became notorious for heroin dealing. A major clean-up campaign in the last decade removed much of this blight and has attracted new businesses. Today Zeedijk is buzzing again with several good bars and music venues and is well worth a visit.

Zuiderkerk (South Church)

Zuiderkerkhof. Church Mon–Fri 1200–1700, Thur 1200–2200. Tram 9, 14 to Waterlooplein. Tower June–Sept Wed–Sat 1400–1800. £.

The soaring tower of the Zuiderkerk is one of Amsterdam's most handsome landmarks. The church was built in 1611 by the prolific architect, Hendrik de Keyser, as the first Protestant church in the Netherlands. Today it is no longer used for worship and houses the information centre for the city planning department. In summer you can climb the church tower. A carillon is rung Thursday 1200–1300.

Café-restaurants and bars

In't Aepjen
Zeedijk 1. Located in one of the city's two oldest houses, this tiny atmospheric café is filled with curios. Go along for the Saturday night sing-song when the city's best-known accordionist, Herman de Neus, plays sea shanties and traditional Amsterdam ditties, re-creating the atmosphere of old Zeedijk, when carousing sailors and press-gangs roamed the street. *Daily 1500–0100.*

Bern
Nieuwmarkt 9. Tel 622 0034. £. A taste of Switzerland in a brown café known for its fondues and peppered steaks. *Daily 1600–0100.*

Brouwhuis Maximilian
Kloveniersburgwal 6–8. £–££. If you're a beer lover Maximilian's is heaven. They brew their own on site and if you ask nicely they may even show you around. The meals are excellent. *Tue–Sun 1200–0100/0200.*

Engelbewaarder
Kloveniersburgwal 59. Tel: 625 3772. £–££. Literary types will appreciate the atmosphere at The Guardian Angel, even though its once-famous literary readings and art exhibitions are a thing of the past. It's still one of the area's best brown bars, however, and the food is good. Live jazz on Sundays, 1600–1900. *Mon–Sat 1200–0100/0300, Sun 1400–0100.*

Frascati
Nes 59. Tel: 624 1324. This snug brasserie-style café of dark red wood, brass and mirrors is part of the Frascati Theatre and serves very good-value food. *Wed 1700–0100, Thur–Sun 1600–0100/0200.*

't Gasthuis
Grimburgwal 7. Friendly, bustling, low, dark, pub-like bar serving a good variety of lunchtime food to hungry students. *Open 1100–0100/0200.*

In de Waag
Nieuwmarkt 4. Tel: 422 7772. The 500-year-old Waag (*see page 50*) isn't weighed down by its long history. In the evenings it's more geared to eating than drinking but the price of a cup of coffee will get you surfing on the internet and it's well worth a visit after dark, when 300 candles softly light its ancient stone interior. *Daily 1000–0100.*

De Jaren
Nieuwe Doelenstraat 20. Tel: 625 5771. The most popular of the city's new-wave Grand Cafés, spacious, airy, light and very modern, De Jaren just about treads the line between trendiness and pretentiousness. Its canalside terrace and balcony are two of the city's most popular outdoor drinking spots. *Daily 1000–0100/0200.*

Restaurants

Kapitein Zeppos

*Gebed Zonder End 5 (off Grimburgwal).
Tel: 624 2057.* Delightful studenty
bar tucked up a small alleyway in the
University quarter. Bright and airy with
a large conservatory area. Friendly
atmosphere, good food, live music most
nights. *Mon–Sat 1100–0100/0300,
Sun 1200–0100.*

(De Schreierstoren)
VOC Café

Prins Hendrikkade 94. Tel: 428 8291.
The interior of the historic Tower
of Tears *(see pages 54–55)* has been
lovingly restored to give a glimpse of
the days when the men of the VOC
(the East India Company) would sail
from here to exotic climes. There's a
wide range of *jenevers* (gins) and
liqueurs including de Zeedijker,
brewed to an old VOC recipe. Perfect
in the summer with a terrace that
looks on to the Geldersekade. Regular
live music. *Daily 1000–2400/0300.*

Café Pacifico

*Warmoesstraat 31. Tel: 624 2911.
£–££.* One of the town's best
Mexican-style cantinas (related to
the London Covent Garden branch).
Daily 1730–2200/2300.

Chinatown

Amsterdam's Chinatown is tiny
compared to those of London or New
York, for example, but fans of oriental
food will still find a good selection of
restaurants around Geldersekade and
Zeedijk. Three of the best are **New
King** *(Zeedijk 115)*, **Hoi Tin** *(Zeedijk
122)* and **Moy Kong** *(87 Zeedijk,
closed Mon)*. The most interesting
Eastern eatery is the highly rated
A Road to Manila *(Geldersekade 23)*,
serving some intriguing Filipino food.

Lana Thai

Warmoesstraat 10. Tel 624 2179. £££.
Many critics regard this as the best
and most authentic Thai cooking in the
city, and there is a lovely dining room
too. You do pay for the experience
though. *Wed–Mon 1100–1830.*

Pancake houses

Two of the city's best and cheapest
pancake houses are within a short
distance of each other in the University
Quarter; **Bredero** *(244 Oudezijds
Voorburgwal, daily 1200–1900)*
and **Pannekoekhuis Upstairs**
*(Grimburgwal 2, Wed–Sun
1200–1800/1900).*

Shopping

Markets

Nieuwmarkt (*see page 50*) is home to a general market, a farmers' market and antiques and curios stalls.

Specialists

Conscious Dreams

Warmoesstraat 12. One of the best places of its kind for mind-expanding substances in the city; magic mushrooms, magic herbs, herbal xtc, souvenirs and psychedelia. Ask for advice before experimenting. *Open daily.*

Jacob Hooij

Kloveniersburgwal 10/12. This splendid shop, in business here for over 200 years and little changed in all that time, is a tourist attraction in its own right, with a selection of some 400 herbs and spices for culinary and medical purposes. Try some of their renowned *drop* (Dutch liquorice).

Warmoesstraat

Once Amsterdam's prime shopping street, this run-down thoroughfare has three very contrasting specialist shops in close proximity, the Condomerie Het Gulden Vlies, De Tulp and Geels Koffiehandeln (*see page 56*).

Second-hand books

The presence of the University means that there are always plenty of thumbed volumes for sale, including many English-language titles. As well as Oudemanhuispoort (*see page 52*) try the Book Exchange and De Kloof, both on Kloveniersburgwal.

Nightlife

Casablanca

Zeedijk. Tel: 625 5685. It was the legendary jazz musician Chet Baker who put the Casablanca on the map, and this legendary venue has recently re-opened with live jazz every night (even if aficionados reckon it is a pale shadow of its former self). On Tuesday and Thursday a complete big band squeezes on stage; on other nights there are varied sessions with karaoke and happy hour between 2000 and 2200. *Sun–Thur 2000–0100, Fri–Sat 2200–0300.*

Theatres

Tucked away between Rokin and the southern part of the Oudezijds Voorburgwal canal, the street known as Nes (it means 'marshy field') is Amsterdam's theatreland, with four venues: Frascati Blincker De Brakke Grond and the experimental Cosmic Theater Most of their productions are not in English, though depending on the type of performance (which is often dance) language may well be irrelevant. See flyers at ticket agencies and tourist offices and *What's On* for details.

Winston Kingdom

Warmoesstraat 127. Tel: 623 1380. This hotel-cum-multimedia arts centre is one of the most fashionable and exciting nightlife venues in the city, with an eclectic entertainment programme varying from Open Poetry Night to Disco Explosion, stand-up comedy to Chicks with Dicks drag racing nights. Club Vegas on Sunday night is currently the hottest happening. *Fri–Mon only.*

Sex shows

Bananenbar

Oudezijds Achterburgwal 37. Tel: 622 4670 http://www.bananenbar.com. It's crude, it's rude and you've probably never seen fruit handled the way the girls do it at the Banana Bar. In between their tricks and erotic routines they act as naked waitresses topping up drinks (included in the price of admission).

Casa Rosso

Oudezijds Achterburgwal 106–8. Tel: 627 8954 http://www.casarosso.com. Not quite so raunchy as the Bananenbar, but still a live sex show, with a high level of choreography. The audience is generally mixed, too. They say there is no haggling on the admission price but if a quiet afternoon show is on then you may get a discount. Drinks prices are reasonable. *Open nightly 2000–0200 (Fri, Sat until 0300).*

61

Amsterdam's sex trade

Like most ports, Amsterdam has offered commercial sex for centuries. But what makes it very different to other European cities is its relaxed social policy towards

the sex trade and its legalisation of prostitution. This should not be confused with organising prostitution, which is still technically illegal, even though there are numerous brothels (referred to as private houses and clubs) overtly plying their trade. There is now talk of revising this law.

The most obvious form of prostitution is, of course, the city's (in)famous window girls who rent their premises much as a market stall-holder does, and become their own window display.

Prostitution in Amsterdam is run much as any other business: the girls (or some of them at least) pay the

> " Plenty of men and women made a concious decision to take up this profession; there are plenty of houses that give a lot of pleasure to their customers in a friendly and positive atmosphere and there are enough customers who can appreciate it. What's the problem then, as long as people act in a health-conscious, friendly and responsible way? "

**Mariska Majoor, *Pleasure Guide*, 1998
(published by the Prostitute Information Centre)**

government income tax; they have their own union, *De Rode Draad* (the Red Thread), and in 1998 they introduced a stamp of approval called *Erotikeur*, awarded to places with superior working conditions and standards of hygiene.

In a survey among prostitutes and clients to formulate the guidelines for *Erotikeur* customers felt strongly about taking their time (no 'rush jobs') and keeping agreements; the girls voted for good washing facilities, clean sheets, obligatory use of condoms, and the right to refuse a customer.

If you'd like to learn more about the oldest profession in Amsterdam (without taking your clothes off), pop into the Prostitute Information Centre on Enge Kerksteeg, between Warmoesstraat and the Oude Kerk, where the friendly female staff will try to answer your questions. For a couple of guilders you can also look into a typical window girl's room, though there's not much to see beyond a mattress, a baby-doll negligée and a wash basin. Of more interest is the Centre's house magazine, *Pleasure Guide*, with price guides for window prostitutes, club prostitutes, private houses and escort services.

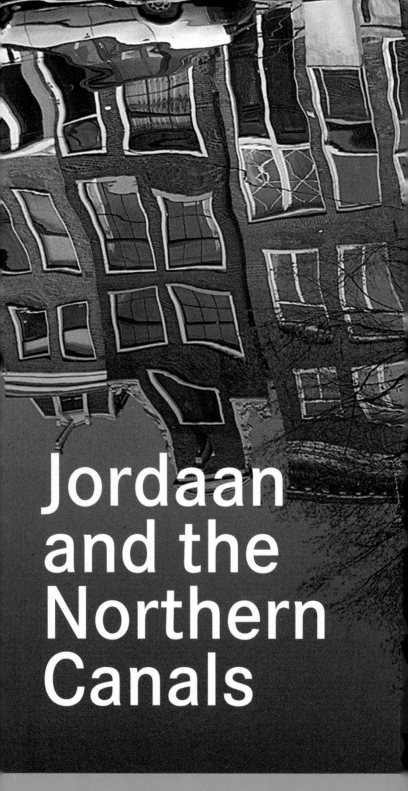

Jordaan and the Northern Canals

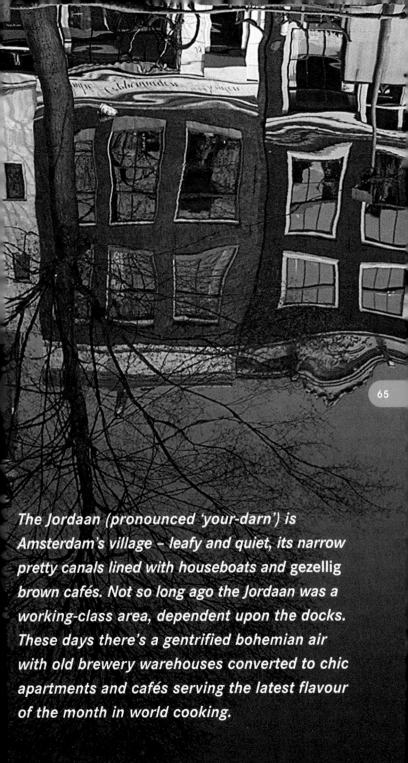

The Jordaan (pronounced 'your-darn') is
Amsterdam's village – leafy and quiet, its narrow
pretty canals lined with houseboats and gezellig
brown cafés. Not so long ago the Jordaan was a
working-class area, dependent upon the docks.
These days there's a gentrified bohemian air
with old brewery warehouses converted to chic
apartments and cafés serving the latest flavour
of the month in world cooking.

JORDAAN AND THE NORTHERN CANALS

Getting there: Trams 13, 14, 17 and 20 go to Rozengracht at the southern edge of the Jordaan, but the heart of the area is only a 5- to 10-minute stroll from Centraal Station and you have to walk to appreciate the tightly-knit streets and atmosphere of this area.

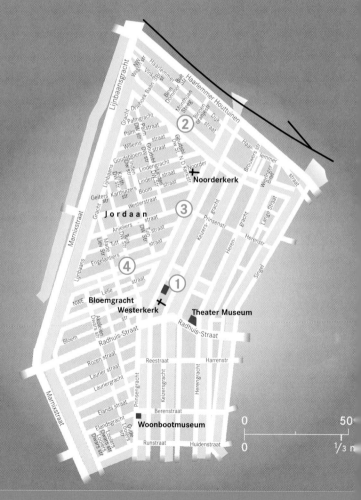

JORDAAN AND THE NORTHERN CANALS

① Anne Frankhuis

This isn't just the story of one little girl, but the tale of Holland's blackest hour. It conveys in very moving but also unsentimental terms both the heroism and mundane day-to-day existence of ordinary people in the shadow of tyranny and impending doom. If you visit only one museum or house in the city make it this one – but get there early as everyone else is making the same pilgrimage. **Page 68**

② Brouwersgracht

It's certainly not Amsterdam's grandest canal but it's many people's favourite. It has a sense of space (a rare commodity in Amsterdam), great views along Prinsengracht, Herengracht and Keizersgracht, and on and around it are some excellent watering holes. **Page 71**

③ Hofjes

Make time to drop into one of the Jordaan's many famous *hofjes* (almshouses). It doesn't matter which one as long as you get to experience the peace and quiet and the timeless atmosphere of these secret hideaways. **Page 73**

④ Café crawl

The Jordaan has some of the best brown cafés in Amsterdam, many within a stone's throw of each other. Particularly recommended are 'tSmalle, Papeneiland and De Tuin, but you'll find your own favourites. Don't miss the bizarre Café Dulac, and if you really want to imbibe the old-fashioned Jordaan spirit finish off with a sing-song at Café Nol or the Twee Zwaantjes. **Page 76**

When to come

The Jordaan is best on Saturday, when the markets at Lindengracht and Noorderkerk bring bustle and colour to the area. It's also a good idea to come in the afternoon, watch the sun set over the Brouwersgracht, and make a night of it here.

Anne Frankhuis
(Anne Frank House)

You can't mistake the Anne Frank House. For most of the year it's the one with almost perpetual queues, though if you come very early or very late you won't have long to wait. From the outside it is nothing remarkable, just another Amsterdam canalside house. Once inside, however, the story of the little Jewish girl who hid here from the Nazis unfolds to become Amsterdam's most moving experience.

In 1933 the Frank family moved from their Frankfurt home and the growing oppression of Nazi Germany to start a new life and business in Amsterdam. Just seven years later, the Germans invaded the Netherlands. Number 263 Prinsengracht served as both business premises and a family home. Here, Anne's father, Otto Frank, conducted a spice business in partnership with Peter van Pels. Storage was on the ground floor and third floor. In fact the windows of the third floor were painted over to stop the light from affecting the spices and so hid the Secret Annexe from view.

In what is known as the Helper's Room, a moving introductory video is narrated by Miep Gees, one of the family's female helpers and the person who retrieved Anne's diary. Except for a few pieces of furniture contemporary to the hiding period in the annexe, the house today is bare, left just as it was when the Franks were taken away.

The family comprised Otto and his wife Edith and their daughters Margot (16) and Anne (13). They were joined by three members of the Van Pels family (referred to by Anne in another version of her diary as the van Daans) and together they moved into the Secret Annexe at the rear of the house on 6 July, 1942, the day after the Germans began to round up the Jews in Amsterdam. In November they were joined by an eighth refugee, Fritz Pfeffer (called Albert Dussel by Anne). The rumour was deliberately spread that the family had fled to Switzerland but the business continued to function and four trusted helpers brought the family food, books and news of the outside world each day. But as Anne observed 'of course we can't ever look out of the window or go outside. And we have to be quiet, so the people downstairs can't hear us'.

The Secret Annexe remained just that for almost two years, until 4 August, 1944, when there came the knock on the door that everyone dreaded. The family had been betrayed, though to this day no one knows by whom.

What happened here cannot be changed anymore. The only thing that can be done is to learn from the past and to realise what discrimination and persecution of innocent people means. In my opinion everyone has the duty to help to overcome prejudice.

Otto Frank (sole survivor of the Frank family), 1970

From the Dutch transit camp of Westerbork they were taken to Auschwitz in cattle wagons. Over the next few months Edith Frank, Fritz Pfeffer and the van Pels family were all killed or died from disease. Anne and Margot were moved to Bergen-Belsen, where they both contracted typhus and died at the end of March 1945, just three weeks before the liberation of the camp.

The sole survivor from the eight people in the Secret Annexe was Otto Frank. He returned to Amsterdam after the war and when it had become clear that Anne too had died, Miep Gies gave him Anne's diary, which had been left behind when the family were arrested.

Prinsengracht 263. Tel: 556 7100. Daily Jan–Mar and Sept–Dec 0900–1900, also 25 Dec and 1 Jan; Apr–Aug 0900–2100. Closed Yom Kippur (20 Sept 1999, 9 Sept 2000). Tram 13, 14, 17, 20. Bus 21, 170, 171, 172. ££–£££.

Bartolotti House (Theatermuseum)

Herengracht 168–174. Tel: 551 3300. Tue–Fri 1100–1700, Sat–Sun 1300–1700. Tram 13, 14, 17, 20 Westermarkt. Bus 21, 170, 171, 172 Westermarkt. £.

The flamboyant rosy-red step-gabled Bartolotti House boasts one of Amsterdam's most striking façades and was built in 1617 for Willem van Heuvel by the renowned architect Hendrick de Keyser. The Italian name comes from a strange request: van Heuvel was bequeathed a fortune by a great aunt and her Italian husband (a childless couple) on condition that he took their family name, so becoming Guillelmo Bartolotti.

Next door, No 168 Herengracht is a handsome if much more austere building, designed in 1638 by Philip Vingboons, one of the foremost architects of his day. It was the first house in Amsterdam to sport a neck gable.

Today the two buildings are home to the offices and museum of the Theater Instituut Nederland and so are partly open to the public. The museum foyer is a riot of rococo decorative detail with flamboyant use of gilt, stucco and large mirrors.

Pictures in stone

Gable stones (also known as cartouches or wall plaques) are a citywide feature, but they are particularly prevalent and colourful in the Jordaan. Predating street numbering (introduced in the 16th century), their original function was to identify the house owner and often his trade. The tradition continues today and a modern favourite is at Lindengracht 53, with an apparently hallucinogenic upside-down world of fish in trees and indecipherable writing. In fact it is simply a clever canal reflection.

You don't need to know a thing about the Dutch theatre to enjoy the museum. On permanent display is a small, dramatically lit exhibition of costumes and a striking, giant glass cube filled with all sorts of theatrical props and ephemera. The museum's temporary exhibits can also be very entertaining. There is a stylish modern café and formal gardens also open to the public.

Bloemgracht

The Bloemgracht (Flower Canal) is one of the Jordaan's prettiest canals and has some particularly fine houses. It's fun to spot the many different gable stones. The houses at Nos 83 and 85 date from 1739, but the most outstanding are the step-gabled trio at 87, 89 and 91, built in 1642. Dedicated to the renowned and prolific Amsterdam architect Hendrick de Keyser (1565–1621), they are known as De Drie Hendricken (The Three Hendricks) and belong to an organisation which has also taken de Keyser's name and is committed to the preservation of the city's historic buildings.

Brouwersgracht

The northernmost of the city's major canals, and the nearest to the docks, Brouwersgracht prospered in the 17th century as a major warehousing canal. Although the majority of Amsterdam's trade came from the east, a reminder of the importance of the West Indies is provided by West-Indisch Huis, the old headquarters of the West India Company, which began life here in 1623, at Herenmarkt.

Brouwersgracht ('brewer's canal') was named after the many breweries which once lined this waterway, though nowadays they are all gone, many transformed into trendy apartments. However, this still remains one of the most interesting and picturesque of Amsterdam's canals. A lively mix of converted warehouses, large houseboats and handsome houses, it may not be as stately as the three major canals of the Grachtengordel but it is much more animated.

Egelantiersgracht

The 'honeysuckle canal' is one of the Jordaan's most picturesque streets, lined with fine 17th- and 18th-century houses. Push open the door between Nos 107 and 114 to enter the Sint Andrieshofje, one of the city's oldest *hofjes* (*see page 73*) dating from 1617 (*daily 0900–1800*). It features a garden and fountain, and in the passageway, antique blue delft tiles. One of the city's most attractive brown cafés, t'Smalle (*see page 76*), is also on Egelantiersgracht.

Noorderkerk

The design of the Noorderkerk (North Church) was initiated by Hendrik de Keyser, though he died before its completion in 1623. A sturdy, rather dour landmark from the outside, the interior is light and airy and its Swiss Cross design means that the congregation sit around the pulpit in a semicircle. Its handsome wooden roof is in the form of an inverted ship's hull and was built in the local shipyards. The church has recently been completely renovated and was re-opened in 1998 by Queen Beatrix.

Adjacent the square of **Noordermarkt** is host to the small but excellent Boerenmarkt (Farmers' Market) on Saturday, which includes all kinds of fresh foods and a second-hand/junk market on Monday. *Church Sat 1100–1300 and for Sunday services.*

Garden memories

Jordaan is said to be a corruption of jardin *(French for garden), a name bestowed on the area by Huguenots, referring to the small market gardens that were cultivated here in the 17th century. Today all the greenery has gone and only canal and street names remind us of the past: Rozengracht (rose canal); Lindengracht (lime tree canal); and Leliestraat (lily street) to name but a few.*

Prinsengracht *hofjes*

Prinsengracht is home to two of the area's better-known *hofjes* (almshouses) which offer a good contrast in terms of size and atmosphere. The biggest is the **Star Hofje**, also called Van Brienen's Hofje, after the merchant

who founded it in 1804. It is said that he did so in gratitude to God for being rescued from an untimely death after locking himself in his own safe! It's grand frontage occupying Prinsengracht 89–133 could be mistaken for a church.

A few doors away (Nos 159–171) is **Zon's Hofje**, much smaller and more enclosed than the Star and much less likely to make you feel you are invading residents' privacy. This leafy 17th-century *hofje* was built on the site of one of the city's secret churches (*see Amstelkring, page 49*) used by the Frisian Mennonite community. Its stone plaque, De Arke Noach (Noah's Ark), neatly indicated its function as a safe haven. Today the *hofje* provides accommodation for some 30 young people and a caretaker.

More *hofjes*

Other *hofjes* worth seeking out in the Jordaan are: **Huis Zitten Weduwen Hofje** (House of the Elderly Widows) in Karthuizerstraat (entrance by No 170), built on the site of the Carthusian monastery; **Hofje Venetia** at Elandstraat 106–138, with a particularly lovely garden; and the **Claes Claeszhofje** at Egelantiersdwarstraat 1e, which also incorporates the **Anslo Hofje**, entrance at 52 Egelantierstraat, known as the Huis

met de Schrijvende Hand ('House with the Writing Hand') for its distinctive cartouche.

Westerkerk

Church only open for services and concerts (see noticeboard for details).
Tower: Apr–Sept Mon–Sat 1000–1600/1800. Tram 13, 14, 17, 20.
Bus 21, 170, 171, 172.

The soaring 85m-high spire of the Westerkerk (West Church),
topped with the golden crown of the Emperor Maximilian,
is visible from much of the Jordaan. The church is the work
of Hendrik de Keyser, begun in 1620, and it is said that to
be a true Jordaanese you have to be born within earshot of
its bells. Like many Dutch churches its sides are a home
for tiny shops.

During the renovation of the church in 1991 bones were
unearthed, believed to be those of Rembrandt and/or his
son Titus. The artist was living close by at the time of his
death and there is a small memorial in the north aisle
dedicated to him.

For a bird's-eye
view of the
Jordaan climb
the church
tower. Try to
time your
visit for noon
on Tuesday
when there
is a carillon
concert.

Adjacent
to the church
are two contrasting memorials
to victims of the Holocaust. The more conventional
is the statue of Anne Frank (whose house is only a few yards
away), looking young and small and vulnerable. On the
corner of Keizersgracht and Westermarkt is the Homo
Monument, a landing stage comprising pink granite triangles.
These recall the pink triangles that homosexuals and lesbians
were forced to sew on to their clothing under the Nazis.

Woonbootmuseum
(Houseboat museum)

Prinsengracht 196 (opposite Elandsgracht). Tel: 427 0750. Tue–Sun 1000–1700. Tram 10, 13, 14, 17, 20. £.

Now moored permanently on a particularly picturesque stretch of Prinsengracht, the Hendrika Maria was built in 1914 as a commercial sailing ship, but has long since been converted to a comfortable houseboat. The term 'museum' is something of a misnomer as there's not a great deal to see below deck, but it's still worth the small entrance fee to get a glimpse of how Amsterdam houseboat dwellers live a cosy, if confined life on the water. Mind your head!

> " *From my favourite spot on the floor I look up at the blue sky and the bare chestnut tree on whose branches little raindrops glisten like silver, and at the seagulls and other birds as they glide on the wind.* "
>
> **The Diary of Anne Frank**

Cafés and bars

Cafe Dulac

Haarlemmerstraat 118. Amsterdam's strangest bar features an amazing Gothic-like fantasy fairy-tale décor said to have been inspired by the works of French illustrator Edmund Dulac and the great Spanish architect Gaudí. Difficult to describe and even more difficult to forget. Live jazz Sundays. *Daily 1600–0100/0200.*

Nieuwe Lelie

Nieuwe Leliestraat 83. A charming, friendly, three-level bar featuring a Cheers-style bar, a pool table below and an area for tables and chairs upstairs. One for chatting and drinking, not posing. *Mon–Sat 1400–0100/0200, Sun 1600–2100.*

Café Papeneiland

Prinsengracht 2. Situated on a very picturesque corner, the Papeneiland (it's name means 'Pope's Island') is a Jordaan institution and the epitome of Dutch *gezelligheid* (*see pages 6–7*). With its huge cast-iron stove, antique blue delft tiles and happy drinkers, you might well think you'd walked straight into a Jan Steen painting. *Daily 1100–0100/0200.*

De Prins

Prinsengracht 124. De Prins occupies an 18th-century property and has all the trimmings, atmosphere and *gezelligheid* of a venerable brown café. It's a surprise, then, to find that it is actually less than 30 years old, but none the worse for all that. De Prins is renowned for its food. *Daily 1000–0100/0200.*

De Reiger

Nieuwe Leliestraat 34. This friendly, popular neighbourhood brown bar is divided neatly into drinking and eating areas and the twain need never meet. Its food reputation is very high. *1100–0100/0200. Dinner 1800–2230.*

Café t'Smalle

Egelantiersgracht 12. One of the Jordaan's most attractive brown bars, this atmospheric establishment has recently been restored to its late 18th-century appearance. It manages to be both smart and cosy, patronised by a 30-something clientele, but get there early if you want a seat. *Daily 1100–0100/0200.*

Café Tabac

Brouwersgracht 101. A spruce and stylish brown bar combining the best of old and new, Café Tabac enjoys a superb location on the corner of Prinsengracht and Brouwersgracht. Short but snappy evening menu. Very lively with a noisy young crowd after around 2300. *Daily 1100–0100/0200.*

De Tuin

Tweede Tuindwarsstraat 13. This funky jazz café is a Jordaan institution, popular with a local arty crowd. Its wooden walls practically exude booze and baccy. Board games are a popular pastime. *Mon–Sat 1000–late, Sun 1100–0100.*

Twee Prinsen

Prinsenstraat 27. Another friendly traditional bar which is essential viewing on any self-respectable pub crawl of the Jordaan. *Mon–Sat 1000–0100/0300, Sun 1100–0100.*

Van Puffelen

Prinsengracht 377. Tel: 624 6270. This very fashionable, spacious brown café is as popular for its French food (moderately expensive but good value) as for its beer and coffee. The rear eating area, with its angel frescos, is particularly pleasant. *Mon–Fri 1500–late, Sat–Sun 1200–late.*

Nightlife

There is little in the way of organised nightlife in the Jordaan, although most bars open until 0100 during the week and 0200 at the weekend. The Jordaan's indigenous entertainment is of the homespun, knees-up variety, practised most famously and frequently at Café Nol and the Twee Zwantjes. You'll either love it or hate it!

Cafe Nol

Westerstraat 109. Don't worry about the dreadful lace curtains and the red light, it's not a brothel. This legendary sing-along institution shows how the Jordaan used to enjoy its working-class playtime before the gentrification of the area. Accordion music, karaoke, yodelling and old Amsterdam songs are rendered by middle-aged crooners sporting hair and clothing fashions borrowed from the museum of bad taste. All well over the top, but in the best possible spirit. *Daily 2100–late.*

Twee Zwantjes

Prinsengracht 114. In the same vein as Café Nol (*see above*) but in a more traditional brown bar setting and much less garish. Live music Fri–Sat. *Thur–Mon 1600–0100/0300.*

Nightclubs

Mazzo

Rozengracht 114. One of the city's best and most relaxed discos with an easy-going door policy. *Nightly.*

Cinema

The Movies

Haarlemmerdijk 159–61. Tel: 638 6016 (cinema), 626 7069 (restaurant). The Movies, established in 1913, claims to be the city's oldest cinema and shows both arthouse and mainstream films in its four beautifully furnished art-deco theatres. It also features a stylish café and a good restaurant, The Wild Kitchen (*Mon–Sat from 1700, Sun from 1400*).

Restaurants

Belhamel

Brouwersgracht 60. Tel: 622 1095.
££–£££. Beautiful art nouveau
dining-room on the canal side where
you can enjoy excellent-value French
cooking. *Nightly 1800–2200.*

Bordewijk

Noordermarkt 7. Tel: 624 3899. £££.
This attractive, highly rated restaurant
mixes French cuisine with Italian and
Asian influences to produce some
original and tasty dishes (each of
which is matched with a particular
wine suggestion). *Tue–Sun*
1830–2230. Closed Mon.

De Bolhoed

Prinsengracht 60–2. Tel: 626 1803. ££.
Nice canalside setting with large
windows and an interior which is
artfully shambolic in a sort of neo-
Hippy way, reflecting much of its
clientele. The food is vegan at lunchtime
with an expanded and more interesting
menu in the evenings. *Daily 1200–2200.*

Burger's Patio

Tweede Tuindwarsstraat. Tel 623
6854. £. There's no patio nor any
burgers here, just a rather odd retro
50s-style dining-room serving top-
quality Italian food at bargain prices.
Daily 1800-2300.

Christophe

Leliegracht 46. Tel: 625 0807. £££.
Classic French cooking with
Mediterranean and North African
influences is the draw at this elegant
canalside house, presided over by
Michelin-starred superchef Jean-
Christophe Royer from Toulouse.
Open Tue–Sat 1830–2230.

Claes Claesz

Egelantiersstraat 24–6. Tel: 625 5306.
££. This friendly place serves what is
probably the best Dutch food in the
Jordaan, casting aside the stodgy old-
fashioned aspects and replacing them
with sharper, lighter, more modern
tastes and presentation. The specially
priced three-course dinner (*Mon–Wed*)
is a popular draw. *Tue–Sun*
1800–2300.

Pancake Bakery

Prinsengracht 191. Tel: 625 1333.
This informal, atmospheric canal
house basement with friendly staff is
a good place to take the kids. Try to
sit near the open-plan kitchen if you
want to watch the pancakes in motion
and see flashes of flambé. Large choice
of sweet and savoury toppings.
Open daily 1200–2130.

Rum Runners

Prinsengracht 277. Tel: 627 4079. If you feel like something sunny to raise your spirits after a visit to the Anne Frank House then a mere coconut's throw away is this funky Caribbean-style café (they also do Tex-Mex). Live music summer afternoons. *Open Mon–Thur 1600–late, Fri–Sun 1400–late.*

Speciaal

Nieuwe Leliestraat 142. Tel: 624 9706. ££–£££. The Jordaan's best Indonesian food, served in semitropical surroundings, with a large and loyal local following. Good portions. *Open daily 1730–2330.*

Toscanini

Lindengracht 75. Tel: 623 2813. £££. Spacious, modern, clean-cut Italian restaurant where everything is made on the premises and you can watch your food being prepared in the open-plan kitchen. The food is highly rated but beware, service can be slow. *Open 1800–2230.*

Shopping

The Jordaan is not really a shopping area. There are no large stores here, or even a concentration of small ones, but there are some nice shops to be found: **Basalt Gallery** at Prinsengracht 112 for ceramics and **Funframes** at Tweede Egelantiersdwarstraat for picture frames are two typical arty-crafty places. Quality not quantity is found here with the emphasis on arts and crafts, books and comics, music and trendy clothing. Noordermarkt is the venue for a flea market on Monday and a farmers' market on Saturday (see page 72). Lindengracht also hosts a good general market on Saturday morning.

PROFILE
Anne Frank and her diary

Anne Frank was born 12 June, 1929, in Frankfurt and died in March 1945 in Bergen-Belsen, aged 15. She was just one of 100,000 Dutch Jews (6 million Jews in all) murdered by the Nazis. Because of her diary she is not a silent victim and has become a symbol of the Holocaust; thanks to her, future generations can at least put a human face and context to all the people living under the brutal tyranny of this dreadful period.

The Diary of Anne Frank was published in 1947 by her father under the title *Het Achterhuis*, referring to the rear part of the canal house used as a living space. It has been in print ever since, has been translated into 55 languages and has sold over 13 million copies.

The diary traces the whole of the period the family spent in hiding, starting a few days after they entered the annexe and ending just before their capture. Despite its child-like appearance, with frequent and touching use of family photographs, as it progresses it is written with increasing assurance and maturity.

ANNE FRANK
1929 – 1945

Central themes of the diary are the boredom and problems of confinement ('it's too dark to read in the afternoons after four ... we pass the time in all sorts of crazy ways: asking riddles, physical training in the dark, talking English and French ... but it all begins to pall in the end'); growing up in such an environment ('who would have guessed that quicksilver Anne would have to sit still for hours – and what's more could!'); news from the outside ('countless friends and acquaintances have gone to a terrible fate'); and of course Anne's feelings, hopes and fears ('cycling, dancing, whistling ... to know that I'm free – that's what I long for'). Just writing the book was obviously a cathartic experience for her, 'for I can recapture everything when I write, my thoughts, my ideals, my fantasies'.

The original red-gingham, cloth-covered diary is on display in the house, alongside its numerous translations.

Amsterdam's so-called Museum Quarter is more
accurately its Gallery Quarter, devoted (mostly)
to Dutch art through the ages. There's a lot to
see, so do it in small chunks if possible. By
contrast the adjacent Leidseplein is virtually a
culture-free zone. It's the city's loudest and most
garish entertainment area, and if you look
carefully there is something here for most tastes.
If you're in search of a more authentic, less
frenzied Amsterdam, walk on a little further to
the attractive Central Canal Ring district.

THE MUSEUM QUARTER AND THE CENTRAL CANAL RING

The Museum Quarter and the Central Canal Ring

ANNO.1769

83

The Museum Quarter and the Central Canal Ring

Getting there: Trams 1, 2 and 5, which run along Leidsestraat to Leidseplein, stop at or close to most points of interest in this area.

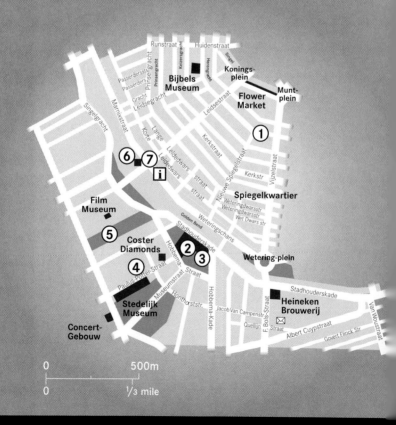

① Kattenkabinett

A cat museum in a canalside house may sound like anathema, but this clever exhibition has transformed the formal museum look of a Golden Age stately home into a cabinet of curiosities. It's a big hit even with visitors who have no affinity with cats. **Page 90**

② Rijksmuseum Golden Age paintings

Think of every Dutch Old Master genre you've ever seen and you'll find it represented here; ice-skaters, still lifes, portraits, windmills, landscapes – painted by Rembrandt, Hals, Steen, van Ruisdael, Vermeer and other greats. **Page 94**

③ Rijksmuseum Asiatic arts

This exotic collection, which stars some wonderfully carved stone figures, is a real breath of fresh air, particularly if you've just slogged your way through the rest of the Rijksmuseum. It's beautifully presented in the museum's glassy, light-filled new South wing. **Page 97**

④ Van Gogh Museum

If you only have the time or patience to visit one of this area's three acclaimed museums make it this one. Unlike the others it's easy to understand, easy on the eyes and easy on the feet. **Page 98**

⑤ Vondelpark

Vondelpark is a great place for a summer stroll (particularly with kids), to get some fresh air, to relax on the café terrace and to watch the various street entertainers. **Page 100**

⑥ Café Americain

One of the city's great institutions, this art deco masterpiece is open to everyone for the price of a coffee. **Page 103**

⑦ Leidseplein

If you're a party animal, you'll love the crowds and hullabaloo here, particularly in summer. In truth it's pretty tacky but some of Amsterdam's best nightlife is also just off here, most notably the Paradiso and the Melkweg. **Page 105**

Best time to visit

The big three museums are open daily, but to avoid queues at the Rijksmuseum and the Van Gogh Museum arrive early and don't go at the weekends, particularly Sundays. If you are in the Museum Quarter on a Wednesday you can break your day with a free lunchtime concert at the Concertgebouw. If a free beer is more to your liking, remember that the Heineken tours depart just twice a day Mon–Fri.

Tourist information

The VVV has an office at Leidseplein 1 (which is actually on Leidsestraat). It provides all the services of the main office (*see page 183*) and is open *Mon–Sat 0900–1900, Sun 0900–1700. Tel: 0900–400 40 40 (f1 per minute).*

Bijbels Museum
(Biblical Museum)

*Herengracht 366. Tel: 624 2436. Mon–Sat 1000–1700, Sun 1300–1700.
Tram 1, 2, 5, 11 to Spui or Koningsplein. £.*

The Amsterdam Biblical Museum merits a visit for its
setting alone. It is situated in two canal houses dating from
1662, built by the distinguished architect Philip Vingboons,
with decorations by Jacob de Wit. Its kitchen is one of the
best preserved 17th-century kitchens in the Netherlands.
Do note, however, that the house is undergoing major
renovation during 1999.

The exhibits will probably only appeal to the biblically
inclined, although the large-scale models of Jerusalem's famous
Solomon's Temple and its forebears are very impressive.

Concertgebouw
(Concert Hall)

*Concertgebouwplein 2–6. Tel: 671 8345.
Tram 3, 5, 12, 16, 20.*

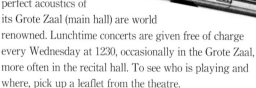

Amsterdam's premier
concert hall is also
one of the city's
most handsome neo-
classical structures,
built between 1881
and 1888. The near-
perfect acoustics of
its Grote Zaal (main hall) are world
renowned. Lunchtime concerts are given free of charge
every Wednesday at 1230, occasionally in the Grote Zaal,
more often in the recital hall. To see who is playing and
where, pick up a leaflet from the theatre.

Guided tours of the building precede the Sunday morning
concert at 0930 (*additional charge £*) and summer concerts
at 1830 (*additional charge ££*), but are for concert ticket
holders only.

Coster Diamonds

Paulus Potterstraat 2–6. Daily 0900–1700. Tram 2, 4, 5, 6, 7, 10. Free.

Amsterdam's tradition of cutting and polishing diamonds goes back to the 17th century, when the city attracted many of the Jewish diamond-processing experts and craftsmen who were fleeing persecution and were proscribed from carrying on their trade elsewhere.

Coster Diamonds is a member of the Amsterdam Diamond Foundation, which has an open-door policy to visitors. In the participating diamond houses you can see the basics of taking a rough diamond, cutting it (which is only possible with another diamond) and then polishing it.

Of Amsterdam's many diamond-cutting houses, Coster Diamonds have one of the best reputations in the city, the jewel in their crown being the cutting of the famous Koh-i-Noor ('Mountain of Light'), weighing over 186 carats and described by a 16th-century Indian Mogul ruler as worth 'half of the daily expense of the whole world'. Presented to Queen Victoria, it is now part of Queen Alexander's Crown in the British regalia. Coster have a replica of the crown on display.

Pseud's corner

Opposite the Concertgebouw, Museumplein is a massive building site undergoing a complete transformation courtesy of landscape architect Sven-Ingvar Andersson. This is what he has to say about it.

'Museum Square is the eye of the hurricane that is Amsterdam in both the physical and spiritual sense. It has always been my intention to make emptiness visible and silence audible – in order to contribute to the creation of an empty bowl, ready to be filled with physical and spiritual vitality which will continually seep out and sometimes explode with the power of a breaking wave.'

In actual fact Andersson's 'eye of the hurricane' will be mostly car-parking.

Golden Bend

Amsterdam's Gouden Bocht (Golden Bend or Golden Curve) is the stretch of the Canal Circle running from Leidsestraat to Vijzelstraat, which was colonised by the wealthiest merchants of the city during the 17th and 18th centuries.

While many of the buildings along here are undoubtedly impressive – the finest is No 412, designed by the renowned architect Philip Vingboons in 1664 – very few hold any great interest to the casual observer. The striking exception is the Kattenkabinet (*see page 90*).

At the opposite end of the Golden Bend (officially just outside it) is Leidsegracht, one of Amsterdam's prettiest and most exclusive canals, lined with beautiful unspoiled 17th- and 18th-century houses.

❝ *These are admirable houses, to my eyes devalued by the swarm of banks, insurance companies and dealers in the drearier industrial effluents who have put their offices here – people who feel the need to put a good face upon their activities.* ❞

Nicolas Freeling (creator of *Van der Valk*) on Amsterdam's 'Big Three' canals

Heineken Brouwerij
(Heineken Brewery)

Sold in around 170 countries, Heineken is probably the best-known beer in the world. It all started in Amsterdam in 1863, when the 22-year-old Gerard Adrian Heineken bought the De Hooiberg Brewery (established in 1572) on Nieuwezijds Voorburgwal. In 1867 the brewery was transferred from the crowded centre of town to the present site and continued here until 1988, when distribution logistics once again forced relocation.

The old brewery is now used for tours which are very popular (get there early to secure your place, no reservations taken). The tour takes about an hour (with a very brief tasting stop halfway round) and also calls in on the shire horses that still pull the Heineken dray through the city streets, though these days it's only for the sake of tradition and promotion. Then it's the part that everyone is looking forward to – free beer! Two tips: take the later tour as you will have longer to sup (around 45 minutes); go on your birthday and you will get a free Delft Heineken mug (but be prepared to prove it really is your birthday!).

No small beer

Did you know that 80,000 bottles of Heineken are drunk in Amsterdam each hour? Or that the company had to substitute its red star emblem with a white star when it exported to America because drinkers declined it on the grounds that they thought it must be Communist beer? (Today it is America's number one imported beer.)

Stadhouderskade 78. Tel: 523 9666. Tours Mon–Fri mid-Sep–31 May 0930, 1100; 1 Jun–mid-Sep 1000, 1400. Minimum age 18. Tel: 523 9239 (no bookings taken). Tram 6, 7, 10, 16, 20, 24, 25. £, donated to charity.

Kattenkabinet
(Cat Museum)

*Herengracht 468. Tel: 626 5378. Tue–Sat 1100–1700, Sun 1200–1700.
Tram 16, 24, 25 to Vijzelstraat or 1, 2, 5 to Leidsestraat. ££.*

The Kattenkabinet is the only private house on the city's
famed Golden Bend (*see page 88*) that is open to the public,
and for that reason alone is worth a view. However, even if
all the other houses on the Golden Bend were opened up it
is unlikely that you would find a more fascinating interior.
Built in the 17th century the house features
beautifully furnished period rooms, which are
liberally decorated with all kinds of feline art
and artefacts.

Stooping to liqueur

*A custom to remember
when ordering a liqueur
in a brown café is that
the glass will be filled
right to the very brim.
You can't pick it up
without spilling it so you
have to bend down to
take the first sip.*

There are old advertising materials, a costumed
mannequin from the musical *Cats*, an ancient
Egyptian cat, African cat masks, Japanese netsuke
cats, modern-art cats, conventional feline portraits
(the most distinguished being *Le Chat* by Picasso)
and many other artworks.

Spiegelkwartier

The Spiegelkwartier is the city's art and antique shopping quarter, and runs from the Rijksmuseum to Herengracht, encompassing Spiegelgracht and Nieuwe Spiegelstraat. The street is as much a window-gazing tourist attraction as for serious shopping, offering many splendid objects similar to those that you have admired in the Rijksmuseum.

As you walk from Spiegelgracht into Nieuwe Spiegelstraat look out for the striking modern art of **Shunyam** at No 72. By way of contrast, a couple of doors down are **M C Gasseling** at No 66 and **Eduard Kramer** at No 64. These two venerable houses make perfect homes for the antique Dutch tiles, old clocks, pipes, pocket-watches and other vestiges of Oud Holland which are their stock-in-trade. On the opposite side, at 45A, **Meulendijks & Schuil** display expertly crafted large-scale model ships that the Maritime Museum would be proud to possess.

In the next block, north of Kerkstraat, fans of the COBRA art movement (*see pages 150–151*) should call in at **Jaski Art Gallery** at No 27-9. On the opposite side there's more COBRA exhibits in **Elisabeth den Bieman de Haas** at No 44.

In the final block, north of Keizersgracht, **Galerie Lieve Hemel**, at No 3A/3B, do things with wood that you wouldn't have thought possible. Opposite, **Den Appel** is a centre for contemporary visual arts, where well-known Dutch and international artists (along with less-famous names) are specifically invited to come and do some weird and wonderful things.

Rijksmuseum

The Rijksmuseum is the national treasure house and houses the largest collection of art in the Netherlands, mainly devoted to Dutch paintings, sculpture, porcelain and decorative arts, but also with important displays of Dutch history and Asiatic artefacts.

The building is a huge neo-Gothic pile, designed by P J H Cuypers, who ignored the prevailing conservative Protestant sensibilities by turning it into 'a cathedral of the arts'. Indeed, its church-like appearance so upset the ruling monarch William III that he allegedly cried 'I shall never set foot in that cloister'. Take a walk round the outside of the building, particularly on the Hobbemastraat side, to admire its lavishly decorated exterior (and also its gardens). If the overall appearance looks familiar then it is because Cuypers was also responsible for the look-alike landmark Centraal Station, though the Rijksmuseum came first, completed in 1885.

Tackling the Rijksmuseum

This should not be underestimated. With around 5000 paintings, some 7 million works of art (not all on show at once), over a hundred public rooms, and a million fellow visitors per year the statistics alone are exhausting. Furthermore, until you get your bearings the layout is confusing, and like all major national museums, it's very likely that room numbers or even whole areas will be closed or reshuffled because of temporary exhibitions, thus throwing the free floorplan that you have just picked up into immediate confusion.

There are various ways to make your visit more rewarding: hire a walkman for an audio tour that spotlights 550 important works; go straight to the bookshop and see what is available in terms of museum trails and guidebooks (*Treasures of the Rijksmuseum* is the most comprehensive for the lay visitor); pick up the free leaflet *A walk featuring highlights of the Dutch Golden Age* or visit the ARIA (*see below*).

ARIA

In the room behind Rembrandt's The Night Watch, *ARIA is an interactive area which includes ten touch-sensitive computers. Extensive cross-referencing enables you to view on screen and learn more about 700 major works of art, catalogued by artist, subject, theme, time, place, technique and so on. The location of your selected work can be printed out free of charge but you need a special card, on sale at the ARIA information desk, to print out other data. It's a particularly good system for children, but get here early to bag a screen.*

Rijksmuseum II

Dutch art

For many visitors the *raison d'être* of the Rijksmuseum is its collection of Dutch Golden Age paintings. Pride of place is occupied by Rembrandt's *The Night Watch* – the Rijksmuseum's answer to the Louvre's *Mona Lisa* – and you will immediately see signs fast-tracking you to this masterpiece. Pause awhile, though, and first watch the 20-minute introductory video to the Golden Age. Then you can either wend your way around the top floor through rooms 201–223 (201–207 contain Medieval art) before coming to *The Night Watch*. Alternatively, you can take a short cut through the eight rooms known as the Gallery of Honour (rooms 230–235) which also leads to the Rijksmuseum's 'Holy Grail'. But either way you should see the whole of the section from 208 to 235, assisted by the highlights leaflet.

Room 209 is where the highlights begin, with Frans Hals's likeably informal *Marriage Portrait*. Nearby are some classic Dutch winter landscapes, with Hendrick Avercamp's ice-skating scene in room 210 a fine example.

Rooms 211–215 feature most of the museum's 18 works by Rembrandt. Probably the best known are *Self Portrait at a Young Age* (aged 22), famously masked by heavy shadow, and *Self Portrait as the Apostle Paul* (aged 61), showing the artist in careworn state. Also notable are the two tender pictures, *The Holy Family* and *Portrait of a Couple* (better known as *The Jewish Bride*).

In room 215 the piercing photo-sharp portrait of Elisabeth Jacobsdr Bas was acquired in the belief that it was by Rembrandt, and it became the museum's most celebrated picture. Later, when it was discovered that in fact the painting was by his pupil, Ferdinand Bols, and not the master himself, its fame was much diminished.

Two more classic Dutch genres are exemplified in rooms 216 and 217. The former houses several works by Jan Steen. *St Nicholas Eve* is regarded as the highlight but most of the artist's paintings are in a similar narrative style, depicting families in a more or less chaotic household setting: even nowadays the Dutch use the term 'a Jan Steen household' to describe a disorganised family. Many of his scenes are light-hearted and jolly, albeit with an underlying serious theme.

Room 221a is home to one of the museum's most charming and best-loved paintings, *The Kitchen Maid* by Vermeer. Instantly recognisable, the blues and yellows seem as bright now as when it was painted in 1660. The only surprise is how small the picture is in real life.

The Night Watch

The subject, and official title, of the museum's most famous painting is *The Company of Captain Frans Banningh Cocq and Lieutenant Willem An Ruytenburch*. Militia companies such as this acted as a combined police force and armed guard in 17th-century Dutch cities. They drew their members from the wealthy upper classes and were pleased to commission such large-scale group portraits from the prominent artists of the day.

What made *The Night Watch* so important was its break with tradition. Other militia portraits are staid and formal; by contrast *The Night Watch* is alive and dynamic. In its day it was hailed as a masterpiece of realism and a study in light and shade, but it was also derided as being disorderly and not meeting the objective of clearly depicting all the militia members.

Rijksmuseum III
Sculpture and decorative arts

The museum's huge collection is organised chronologically in the west wing, ranging from medieval times on the top floor to the 19th century down in the basement. It's an eclectic collection, to say the least, encompassing Flemish miniatures as well as reproductions of whole rooms.

The top floor is the largest and most tiring section. Get through it quickly, and before fatigue begins to set in make sure you see the delftware in rooms 255 and 257 and the striking Chinese interior of room 261.

From room 261, stairs descend to the most popular items in this section, the dolls' houses (expect to queue at busy periods). These ingenious miniature versions of real houses are richly decorated and fully furnished with a profusion of fragile tiny silver and glass objects. Only a handful of such houses have survived and the Rijksmuseum has two examples. They were intended for upper-class grown-ups, never as children's playthings.

The dolls' houses set the tone for many of the 17th- and 18th-century pieces on this floor, which were clearly built to impress. Room 168 features 'the most monumental chimneypiece in Holland' and a magnificent apothecary's cabinet, and other eye-popping pieces of furniture come thick and fast in this section. There is also a large collection of Meissen porcelain. If you make it down to the basement you'll be rewarded with some fine art nouveau and Empire pieces, plus more Dutch porcelain.

Asiatic art

After the fussiness and stupefying detail of many of the pieces on view in the museum's decorative arts section, it's a good idea to take some refreshment (the museum has a good café-restaurant), leave the main building and visit the south wing. This is devoted to Asiatic art and temporary exhibitions, which are frequently of international stature. There is a passage to it from the main building, but unless it's raining heavily you'll probably welcome the chance for some fresh air and walk round the outside to the entrance in Hobbemastraat.

The collection of Asiatic art and sculptures, which has an understandable bias towards the East Indies, is an unexpected highlight of a visit to the Rijksmuseum for many visitors. There are several intricately carved striking stone figures and the imposing 12th-century bronze of *Shiva, Lord of the Dance*, from southern India, is particularly memorable.

The rest of the Rijksmuseum

" *Dutch art is the work of sedentary painters for sedentary townsfolk; an urban art which sometimes paints peasants, but does so with the condescending banter of urban shopkeepers. They are fond of still lifes. They are fond of pictures which tell a story; stories provide entertainment for sedentary people. These pictures were not painted for galleries where people walk about, but for rooms where they sit down.* "

Karel Capek, *Letters from Holland*, 1933

The east wing of the ground floor is dedicated to Dutch history from the Middle Ages onwards, with most space given to the 17th century and Dutch overseas adventurers in the East. In the Drucker extension on the same floor is the work of Dutch artists from the 18th to the early 20th century. Look out for the atmospheric pictures of turn-of-the-century Amsterdam street life by George Breitner.

Stadhouderskade 42. Daily 1000–1700. Tel: 673 2121. Tram 2, 5, 20 to Hobbemastraat; 6, 7, 10 to Spiegelgracht; 3, 12, 16 to Museumplein. Bus 63, 170, 179 to Hobbemestraat. ££.

Stedelijk Museum
(Museum of Modern Art)

Paulus Potterstraat 13. Tel: 573 2737. Daily Nov–Mar and public holidays 1100–1700, Apr–Oct 1000–1800. Tram 2, 3, 5, 12, 20 to Van Baerlestraat; 16 to Museumplein; bus 63, 170, 179 to Museumplein. ££.

Don't judge the Stedelijk (pronounced *schtay-d-lick*) by its exterior. It may look like a perfectly traditional, grand, late 19th-century Amsterdam house from the street, but what goes on inside is, almost literally, anyone's business. Anyone who is anyone at the cutting edge of the modern-art world that is.

The aim of the museum is to present developments in the visual arts of the 20th century, especially those after 1945, and to this end there is a core of permanent exhibits by well-known names such as Kandinsky, Chagall, Matisse, Picasso and Mondrian. More of these are on display in the summer months – in winter they tend to be displaced by temporary exhibitions. By comparison with many of the new works displayed in the Stedelijk, the output of these famous artists now looks almost conventional.

Rijksmuseum Vincent van Gogh

Paulus Potterstraat 7. Tel: 570 5200. www.vangoghmuseum.nl. Daily 1000–1700. Tram 2, 3, 5, 12, 20 to Van Baerlestraat; 16 to Museumplein; bus 63, 170, 179 to Museumplein/Honthorststraat. ££.

The unprepossessing Van Gogh Museum was designed in 1973 specifically to house the Van Gogh collection, and whether you admire its clean lines or curse its bland boxiness, inside it fulfils its function admirably.

The collection of some 200 paintings and 500 drawings was amassed by Vincent's brother Theo, an accomplished art dealer, and was given to the nation by Theo's son, also named Vincent. Most works are by Vincent, but there are also some impressive paintings by famous contemporaries, including Toulouse-Lautrec, Gauguin and Monet.

The earliest pictures are *The Potato Eaters*, Van Gogh's studies of peasant life, painted between 1884 and 1885, which he regarded as among his finest works. Sombre and atmospheric, they were intended to convey the rewards of honest toil and manual labour, though the artist was criticised for showing the peasant's lot as primitive and brutalised.

Vincent van who?

If you really want to know how to pronounce Vincent's surname properly, do as Bill Bryson did (in Neither Here Nor There *) and ask a Dutchman. So, is it Van Goff, Van Go or Van Gok. In fact it's an extremely guttural rendition of the latter, difficult for a foreigner to get exactly right and the reason why the artist simply signed his work Vincent. Over to Bryson:* 'No, no [the man said] it's Vincent Van –' and he made a sudden series of desperate hacking noises, as if a moth had lodged in his throat.'

Vincent's Parisian phase (1886–8) is not represented as fully as other periods since most of the major works of this time are held elsewhere. A perennial favourite of many visitors, however, is *Bedroom at Arles*, painted during one of the few periods in the artist's artistic career when he was content with his domestic state. Another world-famous painting is the vibrant *Sunflowers*, described by Vincent's friend Gauguin as 'a perfect example of a style that was totally Vincent'. In 1986 one of Van Gogh's *Sunflowers* (there are several versions) became the world's most expensive painting, auctioned for £22.5 million.

The final sections of the permanent collection chronicle the artist's tortured state of mind with *Pietà (after Delacroix)* depicting Vincent as the dead Christ, and the famous foreboding *Cornfields with Flight of Birds* (*see page 107*).

St Nicolaas Boat Club

The trouble with most Amsterdam canal cruises is that they operate on the 'more-the-merrier' mentality. If you'd prefer to be part of a small group of like-minded people then try the St Nicolaas Boat Club, who run two open-air boats seating a maximum of 11 people. Because these boats are small they can also go into the smaller canals, including those around the Red-Light District. Beer is served on board and you can take along your own food and drink. Boats leave from near the Leidseplein Theater at 1600, 1800 and 2245. The latter is timed to leave after the Boom Chicago show (*see page 104*). (*Tel: 423 0101 to reserve a place on the boat*).

Vondelpark

Vondelpark open daily dawn to dusk. Trams 1, 2, 3, 5, 6, 7, 10, 12, 20. Hollandse Manege, Vondelstraat 140. Mon–Tue 1400–2400, Wed–Fri 1000–2400, Sat–Sun 1000–1800. Free.

Central Amsterdam is not really blessed with green open spaces, so don't be surprised, come summer, when this attractive park becomes one of the city's most popular spots. It is named after the nation's foremost poet, Joost van den Vondel (1587–1679), often termed 'the Dutch Shakespeare', and was laid out in a natural landscape style in 1865.

During the summer outdoor concerts of every kind, from oompah brass bands to thrash metal combos, are performed on a stage. Roaming the paths of the park are Amsterdam's inevitable itinerant buskers. The days are gone when this was one big hippy commune, but there's still plenty of spaceheads here keeping 'on' the grass.

It's a good place to bring children as there is a playground, ducks to feed and special children's entertainers, usually including jugglers, puppeteers, mime artists and acrobats.

The park is surrounded by grand and desirable properties, including the handsome late 19th-century white pavilion that is home to the Nederlands Filmmuseum cinema (*see page 105*). The museum suffix is a misnomer as there are no permanent exhibits, although temporary exhibitions are occasionally held. The pavilion used to be a café-restaurant and the tradition is still upheld by Café Vertigo (*see page 102*).

Close by is another place that would also appear to be for enthusiasts only but is of general interest. Bordering the park, the Hollandse Manege (Dutch Riding School) is a more modest neo-classical version of the famous riding rings found at such places as Vienna or Jerez. It's freely open to spectators and the best place to watch the horses being put through their paces is from the balcony café (push open the door marked foyer-balcony), which is a delightful faded period piece in its own right.

THE MUSEUM QUARTER AND THE CENTRAL CANAL RING

Museum Quarter

Restaurants and cafés

Pygmalion
Nieuwe Spiegelstraat 5a. Tel: 420 7022. ££. The funky modern colours and décor of this trendy new South African bistro are matched by one of the city's livelier menus. *Mon 1100–1500, Tue–Sun 1100–2200/2230.*

Sama Sebo
PC Hoofstraat 27. Tel: 662 8146. ££–£££. Quiet, restrained setting for what is rated among the best Indonesian food in the city; famed for its *rijsttafel. Daily 1200–1500, 1800–2200.*

Brasserie Van Gogh
P C Hoofstraat 28. £. Bright and airy, decorated in *Sunflowers* yellow, this friendly unpretentious café is a good spot for an aprés-Rijksmuseum coffee, snack or light meal. *Daily 1000–1800/1900.*

Cafe Vertigo
Vondelpark. Tel: 616 0611. ££. A café-restaurant for all seasons: on warm summer days its patio is the perfect place for looking on to the Vondelpark, at other times you can dive into its cosy candlelit vaulted interior, always busy with trendy Filmmuseum types (*see page 100*). The food is recommended. *Daily 1100–0100.*

Canal Circle

Bars and cafés

De Pieper
Corner of Prinsengracht and Leidsegracht. Classic olde-worlde bare-boards drinking den with friendly locals. *Daily 1200–0100/0200.*

Het Molenpad
Prinsengracht 653. Tel: 625 9680. This smart, brown bar is very popular in the evenings for its high-quality food. The walls are covered by the works of local artists. *Daily 1200–late.*

Restaurants

Cilubang
Runstraat 10. Tel: 626 9755. ££. Small, cosy, attractive, long-established Indonesian restaurant. *Daily 1700–2300.*

Iguazu
Prinsengracht 703. Tel: 420 3910. ££–£££. Some of the best South American steaks in the city and a good selection of fish dishes too. *Daily 1900–2400/0300.*

Tout Court
Runstraat 13. Tel: 625 8637. £££. One of the city's best French (nouvelle cuisine) restaurants, run by a famous Dutch culinary family. Its arty, often famous clientele gives it something of a bohemian atmosphere. *Mon–Fri 1200–1130, Sat–Sun 13/1400–1130.*

Around Leidseplein

Cafés and bars

Cafe Americain

Leidseplein 28. Tel: 624 5322. Interiors just don't come any more *Jugendstijl-ish* than the stained-glass, vaulted, hall-like dining-room of this protected monument. Splash out on a full meal or a Sunday jazz brunch (*£££*), or simply take in Amsterdam's art deco *tour de force* for the price of a coffee, while browsing the international press at its reading table. *Daily 1100–2400/0100.*

Café Cox

Marnixstraat 429. Tel: 620 7222. (££). Set in the basement of the Stadsschouwburg (*see page 105*), this laid-back, bohemian theatre café is the perfect place to escape the frantic touristy atmosphere of Leidseplein. Its downstairs restaurant serves a lively mix of Dutch, French and Belgian cuisine at reasonable prices.

Restaurants

De Blauwe Hollander

Leidsekruisstraat 28. Tel: 623 3014. £. One of the quieter restaurants surrounding the Leidseplein and one of the very few places in this touristy area devoted entirely to traditional hearty Dutch food. Friendly, unpretentious, good service. *Daily 1700–2200. No credit cards.*

Bojo

Lange Leidsedwarsstraat 51. Tel: 622 7434. £–££. You'll probably end up sharing a table at this cosy, pretty little rattan-decorated Indonesian restaurant. Their *nasi rames*, a single-dish assortment, is a good, cheap introduction to Indonesian food. Note that the right-hand door leads to the alcohol-free side of the restaurant (the two sides are separate despite having the same address) and that service can be erratic. There is another branch just around the corner on Leidsekruisstraat. *Mon–Fri 1600–0200, Sat–Sun 1200–0400.*

Puri Mas

Lange Leidsedwarsstraat 51. Tel: 627 7627. £££. Excellent Indonesian food in classy surroundings with good service. *Daily 1700–2330.*

't Swarte Schaep

Korte Leidsedwarsstraat 24. Tel: 622 3021. £££. Marooned in a neon sea of mediocrity, the Black Sheep maintains the sort of exemplary Franco-Dutch culinary standards that have attracted royalty. Its dining-room, on the first floor overlooking Leidseplein, is a cosy, typical, traditional 300-year-old Dutch timbered interior. *Daily 1200–2300.*

Tandoor

Leidseplein 19. Tel: 623 4415. £. Set on the first floor overlooking the heart of Leidseplein, this was the first Indian restaurant in the city and is still going strong. *Daily 1700–2300.*

Stoop & Stoop

Lange Leidsewasrstraat 82. Tel: 620 0982. £–££. Gezellig-friendly, candlelit brown bar serving good international-Dutch food. *Mon–Fri 1730–2400, Sat–Sun 1300–2400.*

Shopping

PC Hoofstraat

If you have to ask the price on this designer-label clothing street then you probably can't afford it. **Emporio Armani**, **Mexx** and **Oilily** are among the better-known names. Also **Focke & Meltzer** for the best porcelain.

De Looier Kunst en Antiekcentrum

Elandsgracht 109
The De Looier Antiques Centre is said to be the biggest collection of art and antiques in the country, comprising around 100 dealers in a small warren of rooms. It may lack the glitz of the Spiegelkwartier, but prices are often still sky high – note in particular the model toys. If you want to rummage around junk and well-worn second-hand goods, there is the Rommelmarkt next door (on Looiersgracht), though the prices here also seem inflated. You can always try bartering. *Antiques Centre Sat–Wed 1100–1700, Thur 1100–2100. Rommelmarkt Sat–Thur 1100–1700.*

Spiegelkwartier

When you simply must top up your antique delft porcelain collection or feel the impulse to buy a **COBRA** original this is the place to come (*see page 91*). For a condensed version of this quarter under one roof visit **Amsterdam Antiques Gallery** at 34 Nieuwe Spiegelstraat, where a dozen or so dealers gather together.

Nightlife

Jazz Café

Korte Leidsedwarsstraat 115. Tel: 626 3249. Top-notch live modern jazz is the offering at this atmospheric little Amsterdam institution. *Free. Nightly 2100–0300/0400.*

Bamboo Bar

Lange Leidsedwarsstraat 66. Tel: 624 3993. Blues, jazz and salsa performers tread the boards at this legendary city venue. *Free. Nightly 2100–0300/0400.*

Boom Chicago

Leidseplein Theater, Leidseplein. Tel: 423 0101. Established in Amsterdam for over five years, this likeable troupe of Chicago comedians has already become a Leidseplein institution. Their shows are mostly devoted to lightning-quick improvisational humour with a constant audience interplay, plus sketches on the perils and pitfalls of living in Amsterdam (they are particularly well known for their hilarious crossing-the-tramlines skit). The food is good, drinks prices very reasonable and the service impeccable. Shows Mon–Sat. Dinner and seating begins 1830 (1815 Sat). *Showtimes Mon–Fri 2015, Sat 2000, 2300.*

Bourbon Street

Leidsekruisstraat 6. Tel: 623 3440. Smokey venue with plenty of atmosphere, played by established, up-and-coming and local blues and jazz bands. *Nightly 2200–0400/0500.*

Melkweg

Lijnbaansgracht 234. Tel: 624 1777 (www.melkweg.nl). The Milky Way was once famous as the hippy's hang-out and its in-house coffee shop upholds this tradition. These days it's still very hip, and an eclectic multimedia centre for dance, pop, rock and world music, film and theatre. A glance at a typical month's calendar includes Blondie, a cultural roots extravaganza, a Senegalese soirée, Skank parties, World DJ Battle Championship, Hip-Hop/Breakdance Marathon, Jazz and Fusion. Always worth a look. *Tue–Sun.*

Nederlands Filmmuseum

Vondelpark. Tel: 589 1400. This two-screen film-buffs' cinema is furnished with antique cine-pieces plundered from demolished theatres, including the art deco interior of the Cinema Parisien, Amsterdam's very first cinema. It shows a good range of arthouse and more mainstream films nightly. Free outdoor screenings are held in summer. (*See also page 100*).

Paradiso

Weteringschans 6–8. Tel: 626 4521. (www.paradiso.nl). This long-established former church venue is also a multimedia centre and is the city's main rock concert hall and a leading dance venue. It attracts plenty of big rock names, as well as many other sorts of music. Friday night is the highly popular VIP night (techno-thump variations); twice a month on Saturdays is funk, disco and soul of the 1970s, 1980s and 1990s; twice a month on Sundays is hip-hop. *Tickets available from the VVV.*

Stadsschouwburg (Municipal Theatre)

Leidseplein 26. Tel: 624 2311. Now rather eclipsed by the Muziektheater (*see page 120*) the Stadsschouwburg is still an important venue for opera and dance and hosts the occasional English-language theatre production. It is also home to the Amsterdam Uitburo (AUB), which acts as a general booking and information office for many citywide cultural events and is overflowing with leaflets outlining what's on. *AUB Mon–Sat 0900–1800, Thur until 2100.*

Vincent

Vincent Willem van Gogh was born in Groot-Zundert, south Holland, in 1853. Remarkably he did not start painting in earnest until he was 27, but during the next ten years his output was prodigious, comprising 2000 paintings and drawings. When really inspired he would go right through the night working by the light of candles on the brim of his hat.

Van Gogh began his career in Den Haag, then moved to the rural Brabant province, where he completed his first masterpiece, the *Potato Eaters* (*see page 99*).

After five years in the Netherlands he moved in 1886 to Paris, where his works underwent a major development. Influenced by Gauguin, Monet, Signac and Seurat, he experimented with Impressionism and pointillism and developed his own now-familiar style. Tiring of city life, he moved to Arles in 1888. There he became enormously productive, responding to the intense colours of Provence with some 200 paintings produced in 15 months, including *Sunflowers*, *Night Café*, *The Bridge* and *The Chair and the Pipe*. Personal happiness still eluded him, however.

During this time he attempted to start an artists' commune

with his friend Gauguin, but their temperaments clashed and Vincent theatened him with a razor. Then in a fit of self remorse he cut off a piece of his right ear, and gave it to a prostitute of his acquaintance. Throughout his life Vincent's affairs with the opposite sex had been, almost without exception, a catalogue of disasters.

By 1889 commercial and emotional failure, poverty and overwork were taking a heavy toll. Realising his own mental fragility he checked himself into an asylum in St Remy and continued to paint some remarkable pictures which clearly illustrate his desperate state of mind.

In 1890 Vincent left the asylum and moved to Auvers, but after only a few weeks, during a bout of deep of depression, he shot himself (at the scene of his last painting, *Cornfields with Flight of Birds*), and died two days later.

The Southern and Eastern Canal Ring

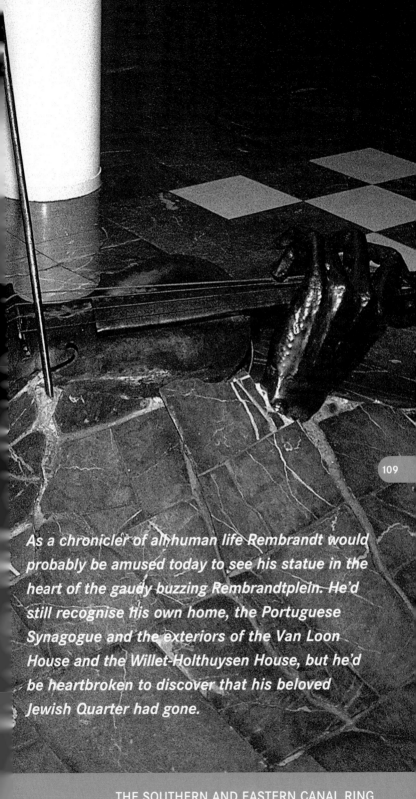

As a chronicler of all human life Rembrandt would probably be amused today to see his statue in the heart of the gaudy buzzing Rembrandtplein. He'd still recognise his own home, the Portuguese Synagogue and the exteriors of the Van Loon House and the Willet-Holthuysen House, but he'd be heartbroken to discover that his beloved Jewish Quarter had gone.

BEST OF

The Southern and Eastern Canal Ring

Getting there: Trams 4, 9, 14, 20 to Waterlooplein or Rembrandtplein.

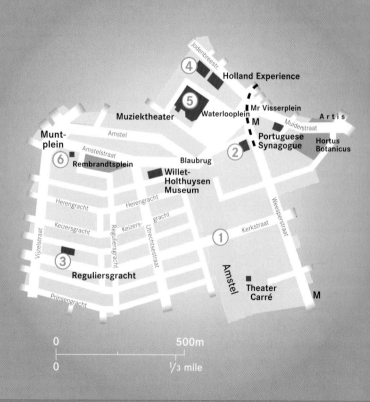

① Magere Brug

A cliché perhaps, but the Magere Brug (*see page 113*) is still a great sight by night, when it is illuminated by hundreds of light bulbs. **Page 112**

② Joods Historisch Museum

This clear, award-winning museum has lots of interesting artefacts. Combine it with the Portuguese Synagogue for a sobering historical overview of the old Jewish Quarter. **Page 115**

③ Museum Van Loon

It's not as impressive as some other grand Golden Age examples but it feels more real, more of a home, and gives a good idea how wealthy Amsterdammers lived about 200 years ago. **Page 116**

④ Rembrandthuis

It wasn't just painting at which Rembrandt excelled, as the graphics exhibitions at his former house will show you. **Page 118**

⑤ Stadhuis / Muziektheater (Stopera)

A modern cultural and municipal statement, or just a monstrous carbuncle? Decide for yourself over a coffee next door in the Café Dantzig. **Page 120**

⑥ Tuschinski Theater

You'll have to buy a cinema ticket for the main auditorium or take a guided tour to really appreciate the finer points of this art-deco jewel. **Page 121**

Best time to visit

Friday or Monday are the only days when the Portuguese Synagogue and the Van Loon Museum are both open. Avoid Sunday if you want to browse around the buzzing Waterlooplein market.

Amstel bridges

The Amstel is the river on which the city was originally built, putting the Amste in Amsterdam. Cut off from the sea since the 13th century it reappears near Muntplein before flowing south.

Unlike most of the city's canals, which only carry pleasure boats – low bridges and narrow width prevent much else – the Amstel still plays an important commercial role, carrying coal and grain-laden ships and barges to the port of Amsterdam.

It's well worth a walk along the river to see the barges chugging to and fro and the workings of the city's famous double-leaf drawbridges as they pass.

Blue Bridge

The busy **Blauwbrug** (Blue Bridge) is a flamboyantly decorated structure built in 1883, modelled on the belle époque-style Pont Alexandre III in Paris. Peer over the bridge to see its boat-shaped piers (best appreciated from a sightseeing boat) and look up at its ornate lampstands, topped by the imperial crown of Amsterdam's coat of arms. The lamps are painted bright blue, in keeping with the original blue wooden bridge on this site.

Skinny Bridge

Much more famous is the neighbouring bridge, the **Magere Brug**, which appears on so many pictures of the city that it has become an Amsterdam icon. There has been a narrow, or 'skinny' bridge (*magere* means 'skinny') here for over 300 years. The name is probably a reference to its original width, which allowed barely more than one person at a time to cross. The present version was erected in 1969. It is the only wooden bridge in the city and is repaired every couple of decades. There are 1400 or so bridges in the city and quite a few of this design (in fact there is one just a few yards away near the Blauwbrug), but for some reason this is the one that has excited the imagination. It's a fine sight lit by night.

The least healthy place in the world

In the bad old days Amsterdam's canals were used as open sewers, as a German pastor recorded in his travel diary in 1838. The stranger who views the city wrapped in a blue mist, and in the autumn breathes its unpleasant odours, will conclude with no second thoughts, that this is the least healthy place in the world.'

Holland Experience

Holland Experience, Waterlooplein 17 (entrances also on Jodenbreestraat and through the Rembrandthuis). Tel: 422 2233. Late Mar–30 Sept 0930–1830 (last show), 1 Oct–late Mar 0930–1730 (last show). Tram 9, 14, 20. £££.

Holland or Netherlands?

To be strictly correct, the Netherlands is the country; Holland refers to the two provinces of North and South Holland. Amsterdam lies in North Holland.

The Holland Experience packs all the visual clichés of the Netherlands into a 30-minute wide-screen simulation film of the kind with which Disney visitors will be familiar. Strapped into an aircraft-style seat you hurtle through the Dutch landscape, over the flower bulbs (a blast of cheap perfume simulates their scent), witness Dutch fun and games on the ice and on the water, then as a finale 'experience' the collapse of a dike. Children might enjoy the show, otherwise it's an experience you could forgo, particularly at the price.

Koninklijk Theater Carré

Theater Carré open for guided tours Mar–late May and July–mid-Dec Wed, Sat 1500. Tel: 622 5225. ££.

On the east bank of the river are two huge landmark buildings. There is no mistaking the **Koninklijk Theater Carré** as its name is spelled large on its richly decorated façade. This splendid neo-classical structure was built in 1887 as a home for Oscar Carré's famous circus – note the jesters and clowns sculpted on the façade. The circus now only comes at Christmas but is still eagerly anticipated. For the rest of the year the Theater Carré is a venue for concerts and musicals (*see page 125*).

To the north, the long dark range of buildings is the **Amstelhof**. It is said to be the widest domestic façade in the city and was built as one of the city's largest old people's homes in 1683. It still functions as such today (no public entry).

Joods Historisch Museum

Jonas Daniel Meijerplein 2–4. Tel: 626 9945. Daily 1100–1700. Closed Yom Kippur. Tram 9, 14, 20. ££.

The Jewish History Museum is at the heart of the old Joodenburt or Jewish Quarter. At the start of World War II, Amsterdam was home to 120,000 Jews; by the end of the war just 5000 remained, and so most of their synagogues fell into disuse. The Holocaust is just one of the many subjects covered by this colourful museum, which should prove of interest to both Jewish and non-Jewish visitors alike and is informative on Jewish customs and practices.

The collection occupies four buildings of a former Ashkenazi synagogue complex dating from the 17th and 18th centuries. The buildings were converted into a museum in 1987, linked together by modern steel and glass structures, and include a kosher café and a large resource centre.

Dutch solidarity

Between the Joods Historisch Museum and the Portuguese Synagogue stands the powerful Dockworker Statue, which commemorates the February 1941 general strike led by (non-Jewish) dockers and transport workers in protest at the barbaric treatment of Jews. The strike, an extremely brave gesture that was quickly broken up by mass arrests, was unique in Nazi-occupied Europe.

Among the many exhibits the most colourful, and probably the most poignant, are the paintings and heart-wrenching story of Charlotte Salomon, murdered in Auschwitz.

Museum Van Loon

Keizersgracht 672. Tel: 624 5255. Fri–Mon 1100–1700. Tram 16, 24, 25 to Keizersgracht. ££.

This elegant canal house was built in 1671 for a wealthy merchant, Jeremias van Raay. Their interior decoration, featuring luxurious panelling, ornate plasterwork, grand fireplaces and mirrors, dates from the 18th century and remains virtually intact. The Van Loons, one of the city's most prestigious families, moved here in 1884 and added, among other things, a collection of some 80 family portraits stretching back to the early 17th century. The family left the house after World War II and since 1974 it has been a museum. Despite its pedigree it is less formal, more homely and has more of a faded charm than its contemporary near-neighbour, the Willett-Holthuysen house (*see below*), with which it is often compared.

At the back of the house is a garden laid out in the formal French style, with a coach house built in Classical style at the bottom. The garden is open to visitors but the coach house is now a private residence.

Museum Willett-Holthuysen

Herengracht 605. Tel: 523 1870. Mon–Fri 1000–1700, Sat–Sun 1100–1700. Tram 4, 9, 14, 20 to Rembrandtplein. ££.

Of the several Amsterdam canal houses which are open to the public this is probably the grandest. Run by the Amsterdam Historisch Museum, it shows how the wealthy classes once lived.

The house was built in 1689 and in 1855 passed to the coal tycoon, Peter Holthuysen. The dynasty and family tenure ended in 1895 when Holthuysen's daughter died childless. She left her home to the city on condition that it should house the art collection of her late husband Abraham Willett, including his delft and Chinese porcelain ware, silver ware, glassware and clocks.

On the first floor is a splendid ballroom and a dining-room, beautifully laid out with Venetian glasses. Up a gloriously gilded staircase is an impressive 'six-poster' bed comprising two joined twin beds. By contrast, in the basement are the plain and simple kitchen with its gleaming copper pans and scullery. At the back of the house there is a garden laid out to a formal French design, as was often the case with such properties.

Portuguese Synagogue

Mr Visserplein 3. Tel: 624 5351. Apr–Oct Sun–Fri 1000–1600; Nov–Mar Mon–Thur 1000–1600, Fri 1000–1500, Sun 1000–1200. Tram 9, 14, 20. £.

This great barn of a building was completed in 1675 as the largest Sephardic synagogue in the world and it remains a very atmospheric place. The massive brass chandeliers are the largest of their kind in the country and with over a thousand candles provide the only light in the building.

Remarkably, the interior has been little altered in three centuries. Quite why this synagogue was the only one in the Netherlands to have remained unscathed, when so many others in Nazi-occupied Europe were destroyed, or at best vandalised, is a mystery.

117

Reguliersgracht

Pronounced re-goo-lee-urs-gracht, this is one of the city's prettiest canals, with a good variety of architectural styles. Look out for the unusual Dutch-German woodwork on the 19th-century houses at Nos 57–9 and 63. The most famous house is No 92, where the painted statue of a stork was erected to celebrate a law protecting the bird. Look down the canal's length and you can count seven bridges in quick succession. In fact, if you stand on the bridge at the junction with Herengracht, you can look all around and see a total of 14 bridges. At night these are usually illuminated.

Rembrandthuis
(Rembrandt House Museum)

Jodenbreestraat 4. Tel: 520 0400 http://www.rembrandthuis.nl. Mon–Sat 1000–1700, Sun 1300–1700. Tram 9, 14, 20 Waterlooplein. ££.

The Rembrandt House Museum is divided into two main sections, the modern museum and the red-shuttered canal house in which Rembrandt lived from 1639 to 1658 during one of his happiest and most productive periods.

As you enter the foyer you get a view of the old house and courtyard where it is said that Rembrandt painted *The Night Watch* (*see page 95*) in 1642, while sheltering under a lean-to. Beware, however, that if you are expecting paintings in the Rembrandthuis, you will be disappointed, as it is dedicated almost solely to the artist's graphic works. Not that Rembrandt's personal life lacked colour, as you will discover during the introductory audio-visual show.

The focal point of the museum is its collection of some 250 Rembrandt etchings (out of a known total of only 290). Although Rembrandt's fame today comes from his paintings, in previous centuries it was for his graphic works (drawings, etchings and prints) that he was known, and these were eagerly sought after by collectors even during his lifetime.

The early 17th-century house in which Rembrandt lived for 19 years has recently been restored to its original condition. Rembrandt spent much more than he could afford on its furnishings, and with its memorabilia and everyday artefacts it throws light on the artist's other roles, as husband, father, teacher, art dealer and art and curio collector.

Stadhuis/Muziektheater (Stopera)

Amstel 3. Tel: 625 5455 (Muziektheater). Tram 9, 14, 20 Waterlooplein. Guided tours (Wed, Sat 1500 ££). Doors open 1215 for a 1230 to 1300 performance.

This huge modern red, white and glass landmark on the bend of the Amstel is a strange mix of city hall and opera house. It was the most controversial Amsterdam building of the 1970s, accused of being completely out of context with its surroundings, a waste of 300 million guilders on elitist pursuits, and the cause of the demolition of the area's remaining 16th- and 17th-century houses (then occupied by squatters).

Violent protests ensued but in the end to no avail and the 'Stopera' complex, as it became known – both a contraction of its two functions, and a reference to the vociferous 'Stop the Opera' campaign – was completed in 1988.

The Muziektheater is home to the national opera and ballet companies (*see page 125*). Its main auditorium has a lovely interior but is beset by severe acoustic problems. It is open for guided tours, though you will have to book in advance for an English translation (enquire at the desk). There is also a free concert every Tuesday from September to June in the smaller Boekman Zaal.

Take a look, too, in the foyer at the remarkable sculpture of a violinist 'erupting' through the tiles. If only the rest of the building had been as imaginative.

Tuschinski Theater

Reguliersbreestraat 26–8. Tel: 626 2633 or 0900 202 5350 (box office). Tours (July–Aug Sun–Mon 1030, ££). Tram 9, 14, 20 to Muntplein or 4 to Rembrandtplein.

Cheap and tacky Reguliersbreestraat is enough to dampen anyone's enthusiasm, so the discovery of the Tuschinski Theater is like finding a diamond in a dustbin.

It was built in 1921 in a mix of art deco, Jugendstijl, Expressionist and Amsterdam School styles and has been described as a 'delightful piece of high-camp fantasy'. The façade is cold, dark and futuristic, perfect for showing the likes of *Alien* or *Blade Runner*. By contrast, the interior, whatever the temperature, exudes a gloriously warm glow with its handwoven Persian carpets, Expressionist paintings, exotic woods, coloured marble, chandeliers, reliefs and sculptures – more suitable for *Aladdin* or *Lawrence of Arabia*.

121

This dream palace was the brainchild of the Polish-Jewish cinema entrepreneur *extraordinaire*, Abram Tuschinski, an egalitarian who believed that all classes of society had the right to spend their free time in such luxurious surroundings. The Tuschinski Theater began life as a cinema and a variety theatre. In 1946, during the post-war period when cinema attendances rose dramatically, it sold a mind-blowing 88.7 million tickets. Tragically Abram Tuschinski was murdered by the Nazis in 1942.

Fans of the original silver screen should note that on the first Sunday morning of most winter months there's a silent movie with musical accompaniment from the theatre's original Wurlitzer organ.

Eating and drinking

Restaurants

An

Weteringschans 199. Tel: 627 0607.
££. One of the cheapest and best-value
Japanese restaurants in Amsterdam.
The open kitchen adds to the fun at
this family-run business. Unlicensed,
so bring your own alcohol. *Wed–Sun
1800–2200.*

Dynasty

Reguliersdwarsstraat 30. Tel: 626 8400.
£££. Possibly the best Oriental
restaurant in town offering a chance to
sample exquisite Chinese, Vietnamese
and Thai dishes all at one sitting, in
beautiful surroundings. Open-air terrace
in summer. *Wed–Mon 1800–2300.*

Kort

Amstelveld 2. Tel: 626 1199. ££–£££.
Housed in part of the 17th-century
wooden Amstelkerk, Kort is a temple
to French–Dutch cooking. You can eat
outside too, on a quiet cobbled terrace
undisturbed by passing traffic.
1200–1430, 1800–2200.

Rose's Cantina

*Reguliersdwarsstraat 38. Tel: 625
9797. ££.* The hottest place in town
for spicy Tex-Mex cooking and ice-
cool margaritas. Always packed; no
bookings but there's a lively bar
where you can wait for a table.
Daily 1730–0100/0200.

Tempo Doeloe

Utrechtestraat 75. Tel: 625 6718. ££.
It's sometimes claimed that this is the
only true Indonesian restaurant in town
and that all the others have tamed their
tastes for Dutch and tourist palates.
A sweeping statement perhaps, but the
food is highly rated here. Do beware
the dishes marked on the menu as hot
– they really are! *Daily 1800–2330.*

Sluizer

Utrechtestraat 41–3. Tel: 622 6376.
£££. Highly regarded for both its
French food and retro atmosphere,
redolent of the 1930s, this fashionable
restaurant is packed nightly. *Daily
1200–1500, 1700–2400.*

Sluizer Visrestaurant

Utrechtestraat 45. Tel: 626 3557. £££.
Some of the best fish in town with
the same atmosphere and quality of
Sluizer (*see above*). *Daily 1200–1500,
1700–2400.*

Bars and cafés

Cafe Dantzig

Zwanenburgwal 15. Tel: 620 9039.
The full name of this trendy newcomer
to the ranks of Amsterdam's Grand
Cafés is Dantzig aan de Amstel, which
you will appreciate best in summer
on its crowded terrace – said to be the
largest in the city. By day it's popular
for drinks and snacks; by night it
turns into a fully fledged restaurant.
*Mon–Sat 0900–0100/0200, Sun
1000–0100/0200.*

Café Kroon

Rembrandtplein. Tel: 625 2011. The
best place to take in Rembrandtplein
is from the first-floor balcony of the
Kroon, a Grand Café in the city's finest
tradition. *Daily 1000–0100/0200.*

Mulligan's

Amstel 100. By universal agreement
the best of the city's many Irish bars
with live bands, story telling, dancing
and good craich every night from 2100
onwards. Mon–Fri 1600–0100/0200,
Sat–Sun 1400–0100/0200.

Ponte Arcari

Herengracht 534. Charming, small
Italian-influenced café in an historic
house on a picturesque canal junction.
Very relaxed with friendly staff.
If you're here in winter try their
wonderfully warming mustard soup.
Tue–Sat 1100–2200.

Cafe Schiller

Rembrandtplein. Its art deco interior
is overrated, but given the paucity of
choice on Rembrandtplein this is still
a good place for a bite and a drink.
Live music on Sunday afternoons.
Daily 1600–0100/0200.

De Sluyswacht

Jodenbreestraat 1. Something of a
sight in its own right, this former
sluice-keeper's house, opposite the
Rembrandthuis, is on a crazy slant
even before you have a drink.
This cosy bar has fine views along
the Oudeschans canal to the
Montelbaanstoren (*see page 48–49*).
*Mon–Sat 1130–0100/0200,
Sun 1130–1930.*

Tisfris

*St Antoniesbreestraat 142. Tel: 622
0472.* Broken ceramic mosaics (*à la*
Gaudi) are the motif of this trendy
café, by the Rembrandthuis, which
serves good wholesome food in the
evenings. *Sun–Mon 0930–1800,
Tue–Sat 0930–2000.*

Tearooms

Backstage Boutique

Utrechtsedwarsstraat 67. Only in
Amsterdam. Meet city icons, the
Christmas Twins, former cabaret
stars whose new vocation is serving
tea, coffee, home-made cakes and the
fluorescent knitwear which they make
themselves. *Daily 1000–1800.*

Puccini

Staalstraat 17. Puccini features the
type of minimalist displays more
usually associated with luxury clothes
or shoes and it may well take a second
glance before you even realise that this
is a chocolate shop. You can see the
staff making the chocolates then go
into the adjacent hyper-modern café to
try them with a tea or coffee. *Tue–Fri
0900–1800, Sat 0900–1730.*

123

Shopping

Concerto

Utrechtsestraat 52–60. The city's most comprehensive recorded music shop for new and second-hand stuff. It's actually spread over several shops, so keep going along until you find your section. Good listening facilities.

Gassan Diamonds

Nieuwe Uilenbergerstraat 173–5. Tel: 622 5333. A member of the Amsterdam Diamond Foundation (*see page 87*). *Daily for tours 0900–1700.*

Waterlooplein Market

Waterlooplein. Want to buy a wooden Indian, a used bicycle chain, second-hand porn videos? Why not try the clothes stalls or the real antiques and curios dealers. Something for everyone and plenty to amuse at Amsterdam's best flea market. *Mon–Sat 0900–1700.*

Nightlife

Escape

Rembrandtplein 11. Tel: 622 3542. This tired old disco has recently been given the kiss of life and is now renowned for one of the hottest Saturday night gigs in town ('Chemistry'), featuring the cream of Amsterdam's DJs. You'll have to wait in line, but don't worry, Escape holds up to 2000 fellow ravers. *Tue 2000–0100, Wed, Thur, Sun 2200–0400, Fri–Sat 2300, 0500.*

iT

Amstelstraat 24. Tel: 625 0111. One of Amsterdam's trendiest and most outrageous clubs, this is just the place if you think you're IT. Take a look at the photos outside to see if you've got what it takes to get in and then choose your night according to your sexual bent (see the board outside the club). *Thur–Sun from 2300.*

Rembrandtplein

The nocturnal focus of this area, Rembrandtplein is a noisy square usually crammed full of revelling tourists and young Amsterdammers. The adjacent Thorbeckerplein is an overspill of this tackiness with strip clubs and **Mr Coco's Pub**, which advertises 'warm beer and lousy food' – you have been warned!

Soul Kitchen

Amstelstraat 32. Tel: 620 2333. If hip-hop, garage and all that techno-thump stuff make you feel grey – or just hurts your head – mellow out here with the funk and soul sounds of the 1960s and 1970s. *Thur–Sat from 2300. Must be aged 25+.*

Jazz and theatres

Bimhuis

Oude Schans 73. Tel: 623 1361. The city's biggest modern jazz venue, home to international and local stars. The more avant-garde, progressive and experimental stuff is taken very seriously here. *Concerts Thur–Sat 2100. Free sessions Mon. No direct advance bookings but tickets available on day from VVV and AUB and on the door from 2000.*

De IJsbreker

Weesperzijde 23. Tel: 668 1805. Pronounced day ase-breaker, this highly acclaimed centre for modern and contemporary music stages some 200 concerts per year, featuring international modern chamber musicians alongside obscure and avant-garde Dutch performers. Although it's a little way out of the centre, on a sunny day it's worth the effort just for its fine café, which has a superb terrace on the Amstel. *Daily 1000–0100/0200. Tram 3, 6, 7, 10.*

Muziektheater

Amstel 3, Waterlooplein. Tel: 625 5445. Home to the national opera and ballet companies with a full programme of opera and occasional dance events at reasonable prices. Free concert in Boekmanzaal every Tue Sept–Jun 1230 (*see page 120*).

Theatre Carré

Amstel 115–125. Tel: 622 5225. Blockbuster shows, top international circuses and national opera companies from all over the world play in this beautiful theatre (*see page 114*). Recent offerings have included the Chinese State Circus, Rocky Horror Show, Grease and La Cage Aux Folles. Best of all is the World Christmas Circus.

Tuschinski Theater

Reguliersbreestraat 26–8. Tel: 626 2633 or 0900 202 5350. You may never again see a film in such glorious surroundings as this (*see page 121*), though you must buy a ticket for the main auditorium. Spoil yourself and go for a box. See local press for programme details. If you don't book ahead, get there early to beat the queues. *Box office open 1200–2000, booking usually one week in advance.*

Rembrandt

Rembrandt Harmensz van Rijn was born in Leiden in 1606, the eighth child of a corn miller who owned a mill on the Rhine, hence the family name. He moved to Amsterdam in 1631 and the following year received his first important commission, The Anatomy Lesson of Dr Tulp, *painted in the Waag, on Nieuwmarkt, and now hanging in the Mauritshuis in Den Haag.*

Rembrandt became the master of the type of group portraits so popular in Amsterdam during this period and his career flourished, reaching its critical apogee in 1642 with the creation of the mould-breaking *The Night Watch* (*see page 95*). However, it was not well received by the group who had commissioned it and their doubts about the wisdom of the sponsorship spread to the wider community. Later that year his wife Saskia died.

The artist was dogged by personal tragedy throughout his life, having already seen three of his four children die in early childhood. His beloved son Titus was also to predecease him, in the same year that Rembrandt himself died.

Following the death of Saskia, Rembrandt had affairs with Titus's nurse and then a servant. This did not endear him to his potential sponsors and he, too, was becoming increasingly unaccommodating. None the less he continued to attract top-quality commissions but overreached himself with expenditure on his home and his art collection and dealing. In 1656 he went bankrupt.

Evicted from his home in Jodenbreestraat (now the Rembrandthuis), he moved into more modest lodgings in the Jordaan. The romantic image of Rembrandt as neglected and impoverished towards the end of his days is exaggerated. In fact, he was almost as active in his last decade as he was at any time in his career and he continued to receive portrait commissions as well as developing other styles of painting. However, he squandered his money and died in poverty in 1669. He was buried in a pauper's grave in the Westerkerk, its location now unknown.

Plantage and the Eastern Docklands

Amsterdam's plantage (plantation) may not be the lush parkland it used to be, but it still provides a welcome break from the city bustle. Seek out its small botanical gardens for the most peaceful escape. Just north of Plantage, the Scheepvaartmuseum is a reminder of what an influential maritime power this nation once was, while to the south the ethnological Tropical Museum features the city's most exotic exhibits.

PLANTAGE AND THE EASTERN DOCKLANDS

Plantage and the
Eastern Docklands

*Getting there: This area covers a wide spread. Trams 7, 9,
14 and 20 serve Plantage Kerklaan or Plantage Middenlaan.
From here the Docklands attractions are a short walk. The
Tropenmuseum is only a short walk from the Aquarium end
of the Zoo, but a long way from newMetropolis. You'll have
to plan carefully if you intend doing the Tropenmuseum and
newMetropolis in the same day.*

PLANTAGE AND THE EASTERN DOCKLANDS

① *Hortus Botanicus*

These gardens are a perfect respite from the city's bustle and feature some impressive specimens. **Page 136**

② *Nederlands Scheepvaartmuseum*

The highlight of this excellent maritime museum is its biggest ship model, the full-sized East Indiaman Amsterdam. Watch its crew going about their daily duties and get a taste of life on board two centuries ago. **Page 138**

③ *newMetropolis*

This is a great rainy-day haven for the kids, where they can push buttons, play on computers and let off steam while parents are upstairs testing their powers of observation, emotional detachment and lateral thinking. **Page 140**

④ *Tropenmuseum*

Swap the grey skies of Amsterdam for some of the world's most colourful cultures, artefacts and practices at the Tropenmuseum. It's not hard to see the allure that the East Indies had for the Dutch. **Page 142**

When to visit

Avoid summer weekends at the Zoo, particularly Sundays. The Maritime Museum is closed Mondays except in high season. Perfect timing for the botanically inclined would be the short period that the Amazonica water lily blooms at the Hortus Botanicus. Note that the newMetropolis adult admission price falls steeply after 1600.

131

Artis Zoo

Plantage Kerklaan 40. Tel: 523 3400. Daily 0900–1700 (Planetarium closed Mon until 1230). Trams 7, 9, 14, 20. £££ (additional fee, ££, for Planetarium).

All the usual favourites are here: big cats, elephants, giraffes, rhinos, hippos, polar bears, penguins, seals, lots of primates and a good bird collection. Don't forget to check your leaflet and the noticeboards for feeding times and other activities, and use this to plan your route.

Near the entrance is the Geologisch Museum (Geological Museum). There are gemstones to admire, a baffling model of the biosphere and a couple of dinosaur skeletons. Close by is a Planetarium (additional charge) with various star shows.

At the far end of the park the Aquarium is one of the zoo's highlights, with impressive large-scale tanks. One of them

gives you a fish's-eye view of an Amsterdam canal, realistic to the point of an old bicycle and a punctured basketball. More exotically there are fearsome piranhas and colourful reef fish to marvel at. In the same building is the Zoo Museum. Its permanent displays are of little interest, but look out for temporary exhibitions, which are often of a high calibre.

De Gooyer Windmill

De Gooyer Windmill, Funenkade 5. Brouwerij 't IJ open Wed–Sun 1500–1945. Tel: 622 8325. Tram 6, 10.

A visit to Holland wouldn't be complete without seeing at least one windmill, so if you're not going to Zaanse Schans (*see page 159*) then make the short bus ride, or long walk, to this landmark mill, which beckons tantalisingly from the bridge opposite the Scheepvaartmuseum.

Rising as if straight out of a Ruysdael masterpiece, the De Gooyer mill dates from around 1664. It used to stand to the south, until a large army barrack block was erected next to it in 1814. As this stopped the wind, the windmill was moved here instead. It recently functioned as a Michelin-starred restaurant and as a bar for the next-door brewery, but disappointingly it's now closed to the public.

133

The Brouwerij 't IJ (pronounced ey as in they) is only one of two surviving breweries in Amsterdam. Housed in a small building which used to be a public baths it incorporates a friendly and popular bar and you can see the 'home-brew' cooking through large windows. There's a short tour of the brewery (in Dutch) on Friday at 1600. (*See also page 144*).

Entrepôtdok

Just behind the zoo, and within earshot of chattering monkeys, the Entrepôtdok is a prime example of how Amsterdam's warehouses have been successfully converted into desirable apartments and work studios.

The dock was built in the 19th century and comprised around 84 warehouses for goods in transit. With a frontage of some 500m this was once part of the largest storage depot in Europe (there is an excellent model in the Amsterdam Historisch Museum, *see page 24*).

Museumwerf het Kromhout

Entrepôtdok. Tram 7, 9, 20 to Plantage Kerklaan. Kromhout Museum, Hoogte Kadijk 147. Tel: 627 6777. Mon–Fri 1000–1600. Tram 7, 9, 20 to Plantage Kerklaan or bus 22, 32 to Wittenburgergracht. £.

> " *...how are they to live in those far-off barbaric regions...? We think most of them will be killed. On the English radio they talk about gassing.* "
>
> **The Diary of Anne Frank, 9 October, 1942**

To see what the Entrepôtdok was like before it was restored, go to the far end and follow it right round. It's not the sort of place to loiter in by night, but by day you should be fine. Walk ahead, weaving left, across Laagte Kadijk, then turn right on Hoogte Kadijk and cross the small bridge to reach the Museumwerf het Kromhout (Kromhout Dockyard Museum).

Founded in the 18th century, this is one of the city's oldest shipyards and is still gainfully employed, mostly restoring historic vessels. Museum is rather a grandiose title for its limited collection of models and oily old ship's engines, but never mind the exhibits, this is all about atmosphere.

Hollandse Schouwburg

Hollandse Schouwburg, Plantage Middenlaan 24. Tel: 626 9945. Daily 1100–1600. Trams 7, 9, 14, 20. Free.

The old Dutch Municipal Theatre, which once saw so much joy and laughter, is now one of the city's most poignant sites. It was built in 1892 and became a leading theatre. In 1941 under the Nazi occupation it was transformed into the Joodse Schouwburg (Jewish Theatre) where only Jews were allowed to perform for a Jewish audience.

> " *The pungent salt smell, the northern maritime keynotes of seagull and herring, the pointed brick buildings, tall and narrow like herons, with their mosaic of parti-coloured shutters, eaves, sills that give the landscape their stiff heraldic look...* "

Nicolas Freeling. Amsterdammer novelist and creator of Dutch fictional detective *Van der Valk*

In the summer of 1942 the theatre was closed down and became an assembly point for Amsterdam's Jews, who were then sent on to Westerbork transit camp. From here they were transported by rail to the concentration camps and almost certain death.

In all, around 110,000 people passed through the Hollandse Schouwburg; only 6000 returned.

Today the theatre is just a shell, a memorial to 'those who were taken away 1940–1945'. A thoughtful exhibition upstairs deals with the persecution of the Dutch Jews, while downstairs is a memorial room and in the courtyard outside, a monument.

Hortus Botanicus
(Botanic Garden)

Plantage Middenlaan 2a. Tel: 625 9021. Mon–Fri 0900–1700, Sat–Sun 1100–1700; Mar–Oct closes 1600. ££.

This small green patch began as a herb garden for the doctors of the city in 1638 and developed apace in the late 17th century thanks to the exotic botanical souvenirs of the East India Company (*see pages 146–147*). In 1682 the gardens moved to their present location. Soon the garden boasted one of the finest botanical collections in the world and was particularly renowned for its medicinal herbs, its Hortus Medicus, which even today draws students of botanic medicine.

The plants and seeds that the Company imported – from South Africa, India, Indonesia, Australia and Japan, among other places – were not only for medicinal use but for commercial trade. The Company carried out pioneering studies of coffee, pineapples, cinnamon and palm oil. The very first coffee plant in Europe arrived here in 1616 and was used to start the coffee plantations of the Dutch East Indies. Similarly the basis for Indonesia's large palm oil plantations was just two plants, sent by the Amsterdam Hortus to Java in 1848.

Over the last few years the Hortus has undergone a major renovation and today the pride of the garden is its Three-Climate House, home to plants from Africa, South America and the Mediterranean in simulated tropical, subtropical and desert conditions. High-level walkways take you above the tops of the plants. The change in climates can be quite startling; spectacles and camera lenses quickly film over, and it takes a good few minutes to acclimatise. In the summer most visitors' favourite plant is the giant Victoria Amazonica water lily, large enough to support a small child on the water. In the smaller Palm House is a 400-year-old cycad palm that is claimed to be one of the world's oldest pot plants.

The gardens are a delightful place for a short stroll away from the noise of the city. Finish off with a relaxing coffee in the old orangery.

Nationaal Vakbondsmuseum (National Trade Unions Museum)

H Polaklaan 9.
Tel: 624 1166.
Tue–Fri 1100–1700,
Sun 1300–1700. Tram 7,
9, 14, 20 to Plantage
Kerklaan. £.

The attraction for overseas visitors of this museum is the chance to admire the splendid interior of the building by 'the father of modern Dutch architecture', H P Berlage (famed for the Beurs van Berlage, *see page 27*). Unless you understand Dutch, all else will be lost on you, except perhaps the museum's colourful collection of agit-prop posters.

Nederlands Scheepvaartmuseum
(Dutch Maritime Museum)

Housed in the imposing Classical-style Zeemagazijn (naval arsenal and warehouse), which dates from 1656, this excellent museum holds one of the world's largest maritime collections and relates the history of Dutch shipping.

Start on the first floor in the 15th and 16th centuries, move through the trade, wars and adventures of the 17th century and learn about the ubiquitous VOC or East India Company (*see pages 146–147*). During this period Amsterdam was at the forefront of world trade and exploration, with some of the finest shipbuilders and mapmakers in the world. On display are romantic maps and globes, the first sea atlases and some wonderfully detailed large-scale ship models, built for practical purposes, never for fun. Finish off this floor with the film about the hardships of the voyages to Batavia (Jakarta), but beware, these were not pleasure cruises and there is one very unpleasant scene (unsuitable for young children).

Take a break at this point, in the museum's excellent café. Full-length windows look out on to the harbour, which is lined with historic ships. Finest of all is the full-scale replica of the swashbuckling 18th-century East Indiaman *Amsterdam*. You are free to wander around the ship, and will soon appreciate how horribly cramped such boats were, even the captain's comparatively luxurious quarters in the stern. Try to imagine what it must have been like with its full complement of 200 sweaty crew members plus soldiers and passengers! In fact the *Amsterdam* has her own replica crew, too, a motley-looking bunch of a dozen or so actors who, from April through October, perform various demonstrations throughout the day, including gun practice (deafening!), preparing lunch, mealtimes on board, burial at sea and so on: pick up the programme of events for the timetable.

> " *I like to wander through the old narrow and rather sombre streets with their shops occupied by chemists, lithographers and ship's chandlers and browse among the navigation charts and other ship's supplies. I cannot tell you how beautiful the area is at twilight.* "
>
> **Vincent van Gogh**

As you will gather from both the film and the activities on board, life on the ocean wave was neither romantic nor safe. In reality the real *Amsterdam* sailed no further than the English coast, where she was wrecked on her maiden voyage in 1749.

On the ground floor, head past the temporary exhibition area to see another impressive full-size ship, the *Koningssloep* or Royal Barge. This stately gilded craft was built in 1818 for King Willem I. Measuring 17m in length it was crewed by 20 oarsmen and last saw service in 1962 during the Silver Jubilee celebrations of Queen Juliana.

Kattenburgerplein 1. Tel: 523 2222.
Web site: www.generali.nl/scheepvaartmuseum.
Tue–Sun 1000–1700, also Mon mid-June to mid-Sept and during school hols. Bus 22, 32 from Centraal Station. ££.

139

newMetropolis science and technology center

Oosterdok 2. Tel: 0900 9191 100 (premium rate line). Web site: www.newmet.nl. Daily 1000–1800 (longer hours during school holidays, call for times). Canalbus run a shuttle service to newMetropolis from outside the Barbizon Palace Tuplip Hotel (opposite the VVV), or it's a 5- to 8-minute walk from Centraal Station along Oosterdokskade. £££, big discount for adults after 1600.

This building, one of the largest and most striking additions to the city skyline, resembles a giant turquoise ship's hull, and was designed by the Italian architect Renzo Piano (co-designer of the Pompidou Centre in Paris). The confidence of the exterior goes more than skin deep. newMetropolis describes itself as 'much more than a science centre ... it is a 21st-century market-place of ideas, a place to stroll and sample'.

Fundamentally it is, as its name denotes, a science and technology centre, with a huge range of interactive hands-on, button-pushing, lever-pulling, mind-expanding activities. It's the kind of place where hyperactive kids and studious teenagers can spend hours solving puzzles, doing experiments, playing games and hopefully learning a little at the same time. But what makes it different from other similar institutions is that it focuses on a much wider range of issues than just science and technology.

PLANTAGE AND THE EASTERN DOCKLANDS

Moored alongside newMetroplis is a collection of some 20 or so historic boats. Caption boards are in Dutch, but if the owners are present they are usually happy to talk to you in English about their prized possession and perhaps even take you on board.

Spread over five warehouse-like floors it is divided into several zones. First and most complex is the area known as The Rings, where you can trade money, information and cargoes in fast-moving computer games. If your childen can crack this area they may be potential City whizzkids. Adjacent is The Factory, which shows the role of tools and machines. Upstairs is The Turbine, where a game of manoeuvring oil tankers without spilling their oil is very popular. The theme of this area is the trade-off between energy use and care for the environment. The House is specially designed for under-sevens to show off their architectural and design skills. Next door The Lab looks a very daunting place, full of technicians in white coats and caps, studiously going about their business behind glass walls. It takes a second, or third glance before you realise that many of these are older children. The fourth floor divides between the rather debatable Science The Debate, and the enjoyable Humanity area, exploring observation and dexterity skills, lateral thinking, emotions, perceptions, prejudices and other characteristics of the human condition.

It's important to realise that newMetropolis is the sort of place where you have to participate to enjoy yourself. There is no language barrier on most exhibits and helpful staff are on hand to answer questions and make sure you get the most out of your visit.

One of the problems that you might face, however, is that at busy times many workstations are oversubscribed. If you think this is your kind of place pay the full admission price (beware, it's costly for adults) and get here when the doors open. Alternatively, come after 1600 when adult prices are much reduced. You'll still get a couple of hours (which will probably be enough for the young children) and towards the very end of the day the centre is quiet.

And finally what (you may be asking) has all this got to do with Amsterdam? Well, free thinking and questioning has always been a part of the city psyche, and the views alone from the café-restaurant roof terrace (open to all) make the journey very worthwhile.

Tropenmuseum
(Tropical Museum)

Tropenmuseum, Linnaeusstraat 2. Tel: 568 8331. Mon–Fri 1000–1700,
Sat–Sun 1200–1700. Tram 6, 9, 10, 14 Mauritskade, 3, 6 Linnaeusstraat.
Bus 22 to Mauritskade. ££. Kindermuseum – tel: 568 8233. Restaurant –
tel: 563 8896.

On the very edge of the Plantage area the ethnological
Tropenmuseum brings a vibrant splash of the tropics to
a grey corner of the city. Like many of Amsterdam's
museums it resembles a municipal town hall building –
only its external decorations, which refer to the historic
activities of the Dutch in the tropics, hint at its contents.
Inside, there is a large exhibition space, with a central
hall and three floors of galleries.

There are eight permanent areas and several temporary
exhibitions on at any one time. Displays focus on the daily
lives and cultural activities of the peoples of the tropics and
semitropics, with a bias towards the East Indies (present-
day Indonesia), but there are also large displays on South
Asia, West Asia, Africa, North Africa and Latin America.
Subjects range from historical studies of bygone beliefs and
traditions, often illustrated by superb masks, costumes and
exotic objects, right up to the less-savoury, pressing issues
of life in the modern Third World, such as overcrowding,
pollution, urbanisation and deforestation.

You can tread warily through a re-creation of some of the slums of South Asia and take a video tour through those of Manila. It's not all doom and gloom, but there is more than enough to give serious pause for thought.

One place not to miss is the museum café, which sells snacks – cakes, biscuits and sweets from around the tropical world. With large leafy pot plants it's a very relaxing place.

In the evening the museum restaurant also serves Third World meals, but check first as it's not always open. Look out, too, for musical events and drama at the museum's Soeterijn Theatre.

There is a special section of the museum for children (aged 6–12), titled the Kindermuseum, but this is primarily a facility for Dutch schoolchildren and labelling is in Dutch only.

Versetzmuseum
(Resistance Museum)

Plantage Kerklaan. Tel: 620 2960. Tue–Fri 1000–1700, Sat–Sun 1200–1700. Tram 7, 9, 14, 20. ££.

" *When to the will of tyrants, A nation's head is bowed. It loses more than life. Its very light goes out.* "

The words on a memorial to H M van Randwijk, one of the leaders of the Dutch Resistance movement

Devoted to the role of the Dutch Resistance during World War II, this museum only moved to its Plantage address in April 1999 and at the time of writing no details were available as to its content. However, judging by the quality of displays at its previous home (south of the city centre), it will certainly be worth a visit.

One of the areas it deals with is that of the 300,000 Dutch who became *onderduikers* ('divers'), going into hiding during the Nazi occupation. The Frank family were the most famous example and this museum is an excellent complement to the Anne Frank House (*see pages 68–69*).

One of the stranger exhibits you can expect to see is the bicycle-powered printing press for publishing *Het Parool (The Password)*, the movement's underground newspaper, which is still published today.

Cafés, bars and restaurants

Most visitors only come to the Plantage and Eastern Docklands area for its sightseeing attractions, as there are very few places to stay and it is also short on eating, drinking and shopping options. However, the cafés and/or shops of all the major sights – the Tropenmuseum, the Scheepvartsmuseum, newMetropolis and the Hortus Botanicus – are all recommended in one way or another (see under individual entries). And, if you look closely, dotted between the sights are various other rewarding watering holes.

Brouwerij 't IJ

Funenkade. Situated at the foot of the De Gooyer windmill, the IJ is only one of two surviving breweries in Amsterdam (the other is the Maximilian, *see page 58*). The name IJ (pronounced ey as in they), refers to the river, but ij also means egg, a pun which the brewery uses in its ostrich logo. Housed in a small building that used to be a public baths it incorporates a friendly and popular bar and you can see the 'home-brew' cooking through large windows. Don't leave without trying a bottle of their Colombus beer. *Wed–Sun 1500–1945.*

Entredok

Entrepôtdok 61. One of the best cafés on the Entrepôtdok, the Entredok has a very *gezellig* atmosphere with lots of old knick-knacks and comfy chairs which belie its comparatively young age. It also serves good food and drink and, unlike many Entrepôtdok establishments, is open all year. *Daily 1000–late.*

Iberia

Hoogte Kadijksplein 16. Tel: 623 6313. ££. Tucked away behind the Entrepotdok the Iberia lives up to its name with an unusual mix of Spanish and Portuguese cuisine. Drop in at lunchtime for a *tapas* or three, while in the evenings you can fill yourself on the house's Spanish speciality, *zarzuela,* a rich fish-and-seafood stew. *Daily 1700–2330.*

Grand Café de Plantage

Plantage Middenlaan. Tel: 421 6061. ££. This smart but friendly establishment opposite the Hollandse Schouwburg is equally good for a coffee and apple cake as it is for a full French brasserie-style meal. *Daily 1100–0100/0200.*

newMetropolis Café

Oosterdok 2. There's nothing very special about what's on offer inside this café but its position atop the city's most spectacular new structure is unbeatable, and there is no admission fee. As long you don't suffer from vertigo take the scenic route, a 120-step walk up the outside of the building. If that doesn't take your breath away then the panoramic views from the roof terrace will. *Sun–Fri 1000–1800, Sat 1000–2100.*

Sea Palace

Oosterdokskade. Tel: 626 4777. £££. This Amsterdam landmark has always been more famous for its floating pagoda structure and splendid décor than for its cuisine. In recent years, however, the food has much improved and in any event this is always likely to be one of the city's more romantic nights out. *Daily 1200–2300.*

Nightlife

Holland Village Theaterrestaurant

Entrepotdok 7–8. Tel: 624 1876. A folklore show in the good old-fashioned 'Windmill-in-Old-Amsterdam' and clog-dancing vein. *Thur–Sun from 1930. Reservations required.*

B&W Café

Plantage Kerklaan 36. Next to Artis Zoo the B&W (Black & White) Café is a large, airy, trendy place frequented by the media crew from the adjacent Plantage television studios. It features live music most nights but of more interest to daytime visitors is its Sunday jazz, between 1500 and 1900, usually of the American 1950s beebop style. You can get a meal here too. *Daily 1100–0100/0200.*

145

The VOC

Sooner or later you will come across the initials VOC, short for Verenigde Oostindische Compagnie, and better known as the United East India Company.

The VOC began life in 1602, when a number of small companies already trading in the East Indies (the islands now known as Indonesia) pooled their efforts and resources in order to coordinate, control and monopolise their ventures. All the spices, coffee, tea, porcelain, silk and other bounty emanating from the East thus became the trading rights of a single body. Most highly prized were the spices, principally cloves, cinnamon, nutmeg, mace and, the most valuable commodity of all, pepper.

The VOC was, in effect, the world's first multinational organisation and for nearly 200 years it was the most

powerful trading body in the world. Its 'corporate strategy' was enforced by its own fleet of some 40 warships and an army of 10,000 soldiers. It worked hand-in-glove with the Dutch state and was even given the powers to declare war and peace.

By the late 17th century the VOC had become synonymous with Dutch colonialism, founding trading posts as far away as Japan and Tasmania, though its heart remained in the East Indies. Its most famous post was Batavia, established in 1595, now known as Jakarta.

Wars with England in the mid-17th century depleted the strength of the Company, and in the end the political and trade ambitions of England and France proved just too much for the VOC. In the early 18th century the Company survived the collapse of the European spice market by introducing coffee to the East Indies, but the telling blow came at the end of the century, when the Dutch supported the Americans in their War of Independence. The British blockaded the Dutch coast and trading posts worldwide. In 1800 the VOC went bankrupt, though Indonesia remained part of the Dutch East Indies empire until 1949.

Further afield

The Netherlands is a small place and there are a surprising number of worthwhile excursions within half-an-hour or so of Amsterdam's Centraal Station (all of the places in this chapter can be reached in less than hour). You want windmills, they've got windmills; you want cheese, they've got cheese; you want tulips, they've got tulips; in fact whatever your preconception of Holland there's a place to satisfy you.

Amsterdam and suburbs
Amsterdamse Bos
(Amsterdam Wood)

Tram service Apr–Oct Sun every 20 minutes 1030–1700. July–Aug Tue–Sat 1300, 1430, 1600. Round-trip £. Bus 170, 171, 172 from Amsterdam Centraal Station goes to both the Amsterdamse Bos direct and to Haarlemmermeer Station. Once at the Bos, bus 70 circles the park.

On the southern fringes of the city the Amsterdam Wood is the favourite out-of-town picnic spot. It was laid out in the 1930s as a work-creation project and today is a beautiful mature space with a lake and over 200kms of footpaths and cycle paths (boats and cycles are for hire). For a history of the park and details of its varied fauna and flora visit the **Bosmuseum** (*Koenenkade 56, open daily 1000–1700, admission free*). The most novel way of getting to the Bos is aboard an antique tram on the special line run by the Electrische Museumtramlijn.

COBRA Museum

Sandbergplein 1, Amstelveen. Tel: 547 5050. Daily 1100–1700. 7kms south. Bus 170, 171 to Amstelveen Centraal Station or tram 5 to Binnenhof, then a short walk.

21 maart 1997 - 25 mei 1997
cobra museum
voor

The COBRA art school was founded in 1948 by three Dutchmen, Karel Appel, Constant and Corneille; two Belgians, Dotremont and Noiret and the Dane Jasger Orn. The name is both an acronym derived from the letters of the members' native cities (ie **CO**penhagen, **BR**ussels, **A**msterdam) and symbolic of the aggressive stance of the new group.

The COBRA artists took their inspiration from children's art, folk art, primitivism and drawings by the mentally ill. Their works are characterised by vitality and bright colours and have gained a wide following.

Barbaric honesty

It's refreshing to hear honest words from an artist instead of the usual meaning-of-life claptrap. Karel Appel, co-founder of COBRA, talking about his style: 'I paint like a barbarian in a barbaric age.'

The modern gallery at Amstelveen is an excellent new home for COBRA, with displays from the museum's large collection constantly changing.

De Pijp

The Pipe – and no one quite knows where the name comes from – is the area adjacent to the southeast corner of the Museum Quarter, bounded north by Stadhouderskade and running west of Hobbemaskade and the Amstelkanal. It is basically a quiet residential suburb but also has something of a bohemian air, home to a large number of immigrants and nouveau trendies.

Running through the centre of De Pijp is the Albertcuyp Market. This is the largest market in the city and operates Monday to Saturday.

Dining in De Pijp

If you're staying in the Museum Quarter the restaurants of De Pijp are conveniently close. **Le Garage** brasserie is one of the city's most fashionable spots, serving adventurous French regional cuisine and international food (*Ruysdaelstraat 54–6. Tel: 679 7176. £££*). At **Beddington's** the English owner-chef serves French cuisine with eastern influences in a designer-interior to rave reviews (*Roelof Hartstraat 6–8. Tel: 676 5201. £££*). At more modest prices try **Karel's** for good café food (*Frans Halsstraat 76. Tel: 679 4836. £–££*). If you fancy something more adventurous go Turkish at **Lokanta Ceren** (*Albertcuypstraat 40. Tel: 673 3524. £–££*) or choose from the large selection of Chinese and Surinamese dishes at **Marowijn** (*Albertcuypstraat 68–70. Tel: 662 4845. £–££*).

Haarlem

A visit to Haarlem is a little like stepping back in time, to how Amsterdam may have appeared before the days of trams and traffic and Holiday Inns. It's quiet and provincial, but with lots to see, including two of the country's best museums, and it's also very close to Amsterdam.

Getting there: 23kms west of Amsterdam. Train direct to Haarlem Centraal Station (13 minutes). Tourist information office, Stationsplein 1.

Grote Markt

Grote Kerk. Open to visitors Mon–Sat 1000–1600. £. Tours (£) Sat 1100, 1415. Grote Markt is a 5-minute walk from station.

Haarlem's central square, Grote Markt, is one of the country's most attractive set-pieces, little changed from the days when it was painted by Frans Hals. Dominating all is the **Grote Kerk** (Great Church), also known as St Bavo's, begun in the 14th century and completed some 150 years later. It's a dark cavernous place and its pride and joy is its huge 18th-century organ, nearing 30m high and one of the largest in the world. In its time it has been played by a very young Mozart (aged 10), and Händel. Frans Hals is buried in the choir, but don't look for a grand memorial; he lies beneath a plain slab.

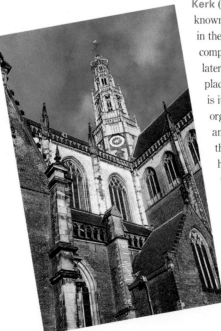

At the head of the square is the **Stadhuis**, the historic town hall, built in the late 14th century, though its present incarnation dates from the 1630s. Its centrepiece is the Hall of the Counts and if there is no function in progress visitors are usually welcome to come in and look around (ask at the reception). It's a splendid baronial hall decorated with 17th-century ancient wooden panels, two-handed swords and other knightly paraphernalia.

Opposite the church is the **Vleeshal**, another handsome historic building. Formerly the meat market, it is now used for temporary exhibitions staged by the Frans Hals Museum. Another hall, the **Verweyrhal**, exhibits modern art.

Frans Hals Museum

Groot Heiligland 62. Tel: (023) 511 5775. Mon–Sat 1100–1700. Bus 1, 4, 5, 6, 71, 72, or a 5-minute walk from the centre, well signposted. ££.

The town's most famous artist, Frans Hals (1580–1666), is in fact an adopted son, born in Antwerp, though he spent most of his working life in Haarlem and is buried here.

In all the museum has some 250 paintings, plus a rich collection of furnishings, ceramics, gold and silver. In gallery 23 this all comes together in a splendid reproduction of the room of a rich citizen, atmospherically darkened and beautifully decorated with gilded leather hangings. Its centrepiece is a rare 18th-century, 1:10-scale doll's house of the kind familiar to Rijksmuseum visitors (*see page 96*).

Like Rembrandt, Hals was a master of large group portraits and there are eight examples in the collection. Two of the most famous portray the Governors and the Lady Governors of the Old Men's Home in which the museum now resides. Also like Rembrandt, the last years of Hals's life were marked by poverty.

Den Haag I

The Hague, as it is known in the English-speaking world, is famous for its court of human rights, and is also the political capital of the Netherlands. It has some outstanding museums and in Scheveningen (see page 158), its very own seaside suburb. Spend the morning in a gallery and follow this with an afternoon on the beach.

Getting there: 60kms southwest of Amsterdam. Train direct to Den Haag Centraal Station (35 minutes). Tourist information office, Koningin Julianaplein, immediately right of station exit.

Well-to-do

Den Haag is a nice place to spend a day, but you're far better off staying in Amsterdam as English writer Matthew Arnold discovered in 1859. 'I never saw a city where the well-to-do classes seemed to have given the whole place so much of their own air of wealth, finished cleanliness and comfort; but I never saw one either, in which my heart would so have sunk at the thought of living.'

Mauritshuis

Korte Vijverberg. Tel: (070) 302 3435. Tue–Sat 1000–1700, Sun 1100–1700. Tram 3, 7, 12. Bus 4, 22. Five- to ten-minute walk from Centraal Station. ££.

For art lovers who prize quality above quantity and start getting itchy feet after the 15th room of a gallery the Mauritshuis is the ideal place. Accumulated by Prince William V (1748–1806), and sometimes described as The Royal Painting Cabinet, it is celebrated for its collection of Old Masters from the 17th century.

Instantly recognisable is *Girl with a Pearl Earring* (also known as *Girl with a Turban*) by Vermeer, a hauntingly beautiful portrait, possibly of the artist's daughter. In the same room Vermeer's *View of Delft* is famous for being an example of Impressionism some two centuries before that school was invented. Equally famous to Vermeer's girl with a pearl is Rembrandt's *The Anatomy Lesson of Dr Tulp*, the artist's first major commission in Amsterdam (*see page 126*). Another favourite Rembrandt hangs here, the self-portrait,

entitled *The Artist as an Old Man*, one of many famous canvases on this theme. Jan Steen figures large with a dozen or so of his allegorical warnings, Ruysdael's epic landscapes brood menacingly and masterpieces by the likes of Rogier van der Weyden, Hans Holbein the Younger, Frans Hals, Peter Paul Rubens, Pieter Bruegel the Elder, Hans Memling and Paulus Potter make the Mauritshuis a Who's Who of Golden Age Art.

Den Haag II

Binnenhof

Binnenhof. Tel: (070) 364 6144.Open at any time. Tours Mon–Sat 1000–1600 (last tour 1545). Closed 14–15 Sept. Tram 3, 7, 12. Bus 4, 22. Five- to ten-minute walk from the station. £.

The Binnenhof is the heart of Den Haag, a romantically turreted castle complex which was once home to the Counts of Holland and today houses the Dutch parliament. Approaching it from the station direction you'll enter the complex by the back entrance, but it is best viewed from the front, where it is reflected in its own small lake called the Hofvijver.

Most of its rooms are closed to the public but the 13th-century Ridderzaal (Knights' Hall) and the First and Second Chamber of Parliament are usually open by guided tour. Tours lead from the vaulted room beneath the Ridderzaal, which includes various historical exhibits.

Around the Binnenhof

There are no less than five museums surrounding the Binnenhof. Across the street from the Mauritshuis (*see page 155*) is the Hague Historical Museum (*7 Korte Vijverberg, Tue–Fri 1100–1700, Sat–Sun 1200–1700, £*). Continue anti-clockwise around the Binnenhof lake, the Hofvijver, to find the other three: Het Paleis (*74 Lange Voorhout, Tue–Sun 1100–1700, ££*), which mounts temporary exhibitions from the Historical Museum; the Prince William V Gallery (*35 Buitenhof, Tue–Sun 1100–1600, £*), an annexe to the Mauritshuis; and the Gevangenpoort (*33 Buitenhof, Tue–Fri 1000–1600, Sat–Sun 1300–1600, £*), a former castle gatehouse, now a Chamber of Horrors-style exhibition. Off the adjacent square of Buitenhof, is The Passage, a grand glass-covered arcade which is one of the town's most prestigious shopping streets.

Panorama Mesdag

Zeestraat 65. Tel: (070) 310 6665. Mon–Sat 1000–1700, Sun 1200–1700. Tram 7, 8. Bus 4, 5, 13, 22. Fifteen-minute walk from the station. ££.

This intriguing 19th-century sightseeing attraction comprises an enormous single painting, covering 120m by 14m, wrapped around 360 degrees. The subject is the nearby seaside resort of Scheveningen in 1881, and the painter was local artist Hendrik Mesdag. You view it from a circular bandstand construction and its 'near-reality' *trompe-l'oeil* effect is heightened by a sloping foreground of real sand dunes, grasses and seaside flotsam.

Haags Gemeentemuseum (Hague Municipal Museum)

Stadhouderslaan 41. Tel: (070) 338111. Info-line 351 2873. Tue–Sun 1100–1700. Tram 4, bus 14. ££.

Recently re-opened following an extensive renovation, the unappetisingly named Municipal Museum is one of the Netherlands' best modern art galleries. It also features a large collection of applied art, and musical instruments.

The pride of the museum's picture section is the world's largest collection of works by the internationally renowned Dutch artist, Piet Mondrian.

Den Haag III

Madurodam

George Maduroplein 1. Tel: (070) 355 3900. Daily 0900–1700, late Mar–late Jun until 2000, Jul–Aug until 2200. Tram 1, 9, bus 22, 65. Five-minute walk from Haags Gemeentemuseum. £££.

Madurodam is the Netherlands in miniature, a 1:25 scale reproduction of hundreds of well-known landmarks and scenes including the Alkmaar Cheese Market, Dam Square, windmills, canals and dikes galore. It's very popular with children and adults alike, particularly when it is illuminated by night during the summer.

Scheveningen

The country's top seaside resort, Scheveningen nowadays merges almost seamlessly with Den Haag. It's only 4kms from Den Haag railway station to the coast and so is easily managed in a day-trip from Amsterdam.

Scheveningen was a fashionable spa resort in the 19th century and the centre is still known as Scheveningen Bad, though the Kurhaus, a grand Empire-style hotel, is the only reminder of its gracious past. Today Scheveningen is a typical commercialised mass-market seaside resort, famed for its excellent sandy beach, which gets very crowded in summer. Also worth a visit is the Sea Life Aquarium (*13 Strandweg; daily 1000–1800, Jul–Aug 1000–2000. ££*), the Statues of the Sea Museum (*1 Harteveltstraat, Tue–Sun 1100–1700. £*) and the Scheveningen Museum (*summer Mon–Sat 1000–1700, winter Tue–Sat 1000–1600. £*). If you want to see exactly what Scheveningen looked like 100 years ago visit the Panorama Mesdag (*see page 157*).

Windmills

When Monet came to paint the Zaanse Schaans landscape in the 1870s there were over 1000 windmills in this area alone, producing corn, mustard, paint pigments and vegetable oil, and being used as sawmills (as they were in the Amsterdam shipyards). The country's windmill population peaked in the 1850s with 9000 windmills recorded. Today there are around 900 still in good condition and 500 still working.

Zaanse Schans

*Zaanse Schaans Village, Schansend 1. Tel: (075) 616 2221. Daily 0830–1800,
summer until 1700. Windmills and craft exhibitions open Mar–Oct Tue–Sun
1000–1700, Nov–Feb Sat–Sun 1000–1700. If you don't have the Rail Idee
pass (see below) there is a separate entrance charge (£) per mill or workshop.*

Zaanse Schans is a large open-air museum-cum-reconstructed
village formed in 1960, when a number of windmills and
historic buildings, many from the 17th century, were moved
here from various parts of the country in order to save them
from destruction. Enthusiasts live in the mills and are keen
to share their knowledge with interested visitors and to
demonstrate the workings of their antique charges.

In other buildings craft workshops and period rooms are open
to visitors and from March to October you can take a scenic
boat trip along the River Zaan alongside many of the mills.

A short walk away at Koog aan de Zaan station, the
Molenmuseum (Windmill Museum) will fill you in on the
historical importance of Holland's most distinctive landmarks.

A Rail Idee ticket from the VVV in Amsterdam includes the
return train journey to Koog Zaandijk (13kms north), a boat
cruise and entrance to all buildings.

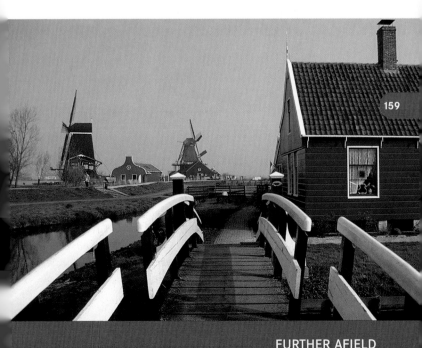

159

FURTHER AFIELD

PROFILE

More trips out of Amsterdam

Alkmaar

You've seen the postcards of the traditional cheese market, but what they don't convey is the bustle and festive atmosphere. Antiques and craft stalls abound and the town also has several fine 15th- and 16th-century buildings to visit.

When to go: mid-April–mid-Sept 1000–1200 (arrive early to get a good place).

Delft

They've been making the famous blue-and-white porcelain here for over 300 years, none longer than De Porceleyne Fles factory who let visitors in on some of their secrets. There's more antique porcelain at Huis Lambert van Meerten Museum, but Delft is definitely more than a one-product town. Do not miss the Prinsenhof Museum.

When to go: Mon–Sat.

Edam

Edam may be famous for cheese, but unlike some places here it is not overhyped. The Kaasmarkt is open daily in summer although it doesn't have the razzmatazz of Alkmaar or Gouda. The town is quiet and calm and the Edams Museum, a labyrinth of small dark rooms, is a delightful place.

When to go: anytime during the summer.

Gouda

Gouda has another traditional cheese market, set against the backdrop of the 15th-century town hall. In the quiet cobbled lanes of the medieval quarter you'll find St Janskerk with the best stained glass in the Netherlands, and opposite is the Catharina Gasthuis, now home to a fine collection of art through the ages.

When to go: Cheese market late Jun–late Aug Thur 0930–1200.

Keukenhof

Famous as the home of the Dutch bulb fields, each spring Keukenhof lays on the 'greatest flower show on earth'.

The climax is at the end of April, when a huge flower parade takes place in neighbouring Lisse. A great sight, but it can be horribly crowded.

When to go: late March to the end of May.

Marken

An old-world Holland of pristine clapboard houses on stilts and local people in traditional costume, Marken is marred by crowds and commercialism, but not as badly as neighbouring Volendam. Catch the boat to nearby Monnickendam for another picture-postcard village.

When to go: Oct–May to avoid the crowds.

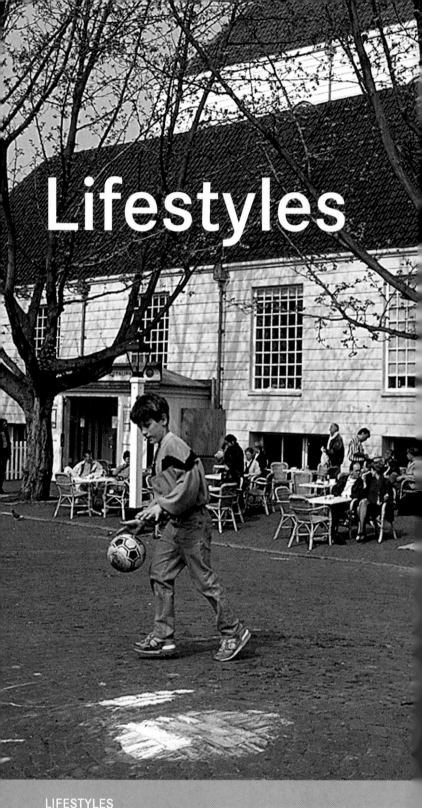

Lifestyles

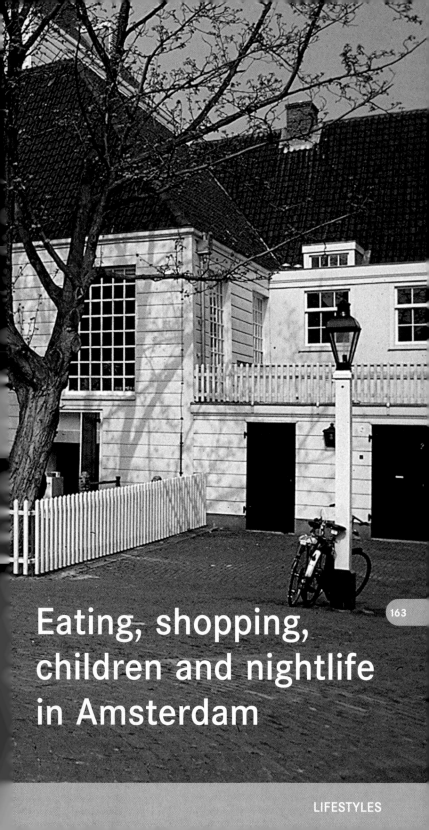

Eating, shopping, children and nightlife in Amsterdam

Eating out

Amsterdam's indigenous Dutch food is basically from the meat-and-two-veg school of cooking. It is nothing to write home about, but it is always hearty, usually tasty and, particularly in the winter, can be very satisfying. This heavy style of cooking is leavened by seafood from the North Sea and Zuiderzee, although only the humble herring makes an impression on most visitors.

The city's imported restaurants are a very different prospect. The most popular foreign cuisine is Indonesian, the most critically acclaimed is French, but you can eat your way round much of the world from Argentina to the West Indies via South Africa and Surinam.

Most restaurants are informal and *gezellig* (*see pages 6–7*) with candles and plain wooden furniture a common style in the budget-to-moderate price range. This is particularly the case in Amsterdam's many brown cafés (*see page 174*), most of which have now completely blurred the lines between eating and drinking.

Evening meals start early, around 1800, and generally finish around 2200. It's best to book ahead at all times of the year as the popular places are often oversubscribed.

Beware, Amsterdam is not a cheap place to eat out but the quality and service is invariably very good. Tipping (*see page 189*) is not part of the culture so don't feel obliged to leave the usual 10 per cent.

Dining out used to be cash-only, but things have changed. The higher the prices the more chance there is that the establishment will take credit cards, but always check first.

Meat and veg

Erwtensoep (Dutch pea soup) is a mini-meal in itself. This delicious green-brown split-pea broth is flavoured with smoked bacon, sausage and/or pork and is traditionally served with a slice of dark, heavy sweet rye bread (*roggerbrood*), perhaps topped with cured ham (*kalenspek*).

Hutspot is a stew or hotpot of meat (usually beef) and vegetables, *stamppot* is a similar meal with smoked sausage.

Fish and seafood

The most famous Dutch fish dish is marinated raw herring (*harring*), traditionally served in a soft white roll with onions and sweet cucumber pickle. Best is *nieuwe harring*, a mild-tasting young fish, available in spring. Herring is a street food, served at stalls, never in restaurants.

Other take-away treats include smoked eel (*gerookte paling*) and more familiarly, cod, salmon and prawns.

From around September to April steaming great bowls of mussels (*mosselen*), spawned in the Zuiderzee, make diners' eyes light up in restaurants and brown cafés.

Pancakes

A Dutch speciality, pancakes (*pannekoeken*) are served both sweet and savoury, with a multitude of fillings. They are always a good bet for a budget meal.

Some cafés offer *poffertjes*, small, sweet, thick pancakes, liberally dusted with icing sugar and dripping with butter. These are delicious but beware – they can be surprisingly expensive.

Snacks and street food

For lunch an *uitsmijter* is a traditional snack of an open meat sandwich topped with a fried egg. The bread is usually the white processed variety and the whole thing is disappointingly bland. More satisfying is a *belegde broodje* (filled roll).

Kroketten or *bitterballen* are deep-fried meat or cheese croquettes, served with a sweet mustard. They are delicious, if rather rich, and can be quite expensive. *Frikadellen* are spicy minced-meat balls.

Apart from herring (*see above*) the ubiquitous indigenous street food is chips, often advertised as *Vlaamse frites* ('Flemish fries'), which are supposedly the best kind. The traditional accompaniment is mayonnaise but you can have ketchup, curry sauce or any one of a variety of accompaniments.

Eastern foods, notably *falafels* and *kebabs* (the latter referred to as *schwarmas* or *shoarmas*) are common too.

Cheese

Dutch cheese *(kaas)* need not be of the bland Edam and Gouda variety with which most foreigners are familiar. For more taste look for maturity – *jong* is young, *belegen* is matured and *oud* is old; pungent and strong. The Dutch are also very fond of *fondues*.

Indonesian food

As the English love Indian food so the Dutch have a passion for Indonesian cooking. The best way to get acquainted is to order a *rijsttafel*. It means rice table and comprises anything up to 20 small dishes shared between two people. Typical dishes are: *beef rendang* (in a spicy red sauce), *chicken satay* (in a spicy peanut sauce), *gado gado* (vegetables and boiled egg with peanut sauce), *bami goreng* (fried noodles with various meats and vegetables), *nasi goreng* (fried rice with various meats and vegetables), perhaps *cummi cummi* (squid) and steamed white rice. Spiciness ranges from delicate to mouth-searing, though most tourist restaurants err on the mild side. If you think you would like a bit of extra heat ask the waiter for advice. One thing that is always hot is the red chilli *sambal* pickle.

If you are dining alone, or a *rijsttafel* seems too daunting or expensive, you may be able to get a *nasi rames*, which is a small variety of dishes on a single plate. Avoid Chinese-Indonesian hybrid restaurants unless you want a similar hybrid cuisine.

Drinks

Tea and coffee

Ask simply for a coffee and you will get a cup of black coffee with a little tub of *koffiemelk*. A *kafe verkeerd* is a weak coffee made with milk. Most places do capuccino and espresso.

Tea is generally a cup of boiling water and your own choice of various flavoured teabags. You always have to ask for milk.

Beer

The Dutch take their beer very seriously, with Amstel and Heineken the leading brands. If you just ask for a beer you will get the traditional golden-coloured pils, but there are dark beers too. In early winter try the delicious sweet dark *bokbier*; by late December it has gone. In summer *witbier*, literally white beer, brewed from wheat, is a traditional thirst quencher, though it is available all year round.

Jenever

Jenever (pronounced jen-ever), also known as *Hollands*, is gin flavoured with juniper berries. The standard (*yong*) *jenever* is usually mixed (with cola, tonic etc), but *oud jenever*, oily and pungent, is drunk straight.

Shopping

Amsterdam is not a great shopping city in the conventional sense. Compared to many major European cities its department stores and open-air markets are mediocre, and prices across the board are generally expensive. Where the city does score is in its small, high-quality, individual specialist shops. Window displays are often created with flair and panache, making browsing as much fun as buying.

Malls and precincts

Amsterdam has not really embraced the American concept of shopping under a single roof. However, its principal exception, **Magna Plaza** (*see page 31*), is both a commercial and aesthetic success, and the latest mall, **Kalverstoren**, also bodes well. Ugly, characterless, pedestrianised Kalverstraat makes up the city's main shopping artery (*see page 39*).

It's worth remembering that Schiphol airport has a very good selection of shops, though only duty-free goods are likely to be competitively priced.

Side-streets

You'll find some of the most interesting small shops in the narrow side-streets between the major canals. These tend to cluster here as historically commercial enterprises were not allowed next to the grand canalside dwellings. Some of the

best of these streets lie between Leidsegracht and Rozengracht, Reestraat and Hartenstraat, Runstraat and Huidenstraat, and Berenstraat and Wolvenstraat. Due south off Rembrandtplein, Utrechtsestraat is acclaimed as one of the city's most up-and-coming streets, with lots of trendy shops and eating places. This in turn is crossed by Kerkstraat (running parallel to, and in between Keizersgracht and Prinsengracht), also with good shops.

What to buy

Art and antiques

Go to the Spiegelkwartier (*see page 91*) for the best selection and displays, if not the keenest prices. You might find more bargains at the De Looier Antiekcentrum (*see page 104*), though prices can be very steep here too. It encompasses a *Rommelmarkt* (junk market), though the best flea market is at Waterlooplein (*see page 124*). One of the city's favourite cheap antique shops is the photogenic 't Winkeltje at Prinsengracht 228.

If your budget only runs to postcards and posters, try Art Unlimited whose main store covers three floors at Keizersgracht 510. It boasts the largest collection of art and photography reproductions in Holland and also has a Postcard Gallery on Max Euweplein, near Leidseplein.

Books

Amsterdammers are voracious readers and there is always a huge volume of English titles, both new and second-hand, on the shelves. The city is spoilt for good bookshops. For more eclectic titles look around the main university buildings on Spui (*see page 35*) and just south of the Red-Light District (*see pages 52–53*). The museum shops are good for specialist titles.

Confectionery

Droste and Van Houten chocolates are always welcome as a gift and you'll get the full range in Amsterdam. Beware though, Droste are widely exported and you'll probably be able to buy them more cheaply at home.

Handmade Belgian chocolates are another ever-popular, albeit expensive treat (Leonidas have their own shop on Damstraat). The grand old dame of Amsterdam's confectionery creators is Patisserie Pompadour, on Huidenstraat, with 45 varieties of handmade chocolates, though Puccini (*see page 123*) is snapping at their heels.

For a more unusual type of confectionery try one of the 38 varieties of *drop*, Dutch liquorice, from Jacob Hooy's wonderfully old-fashioned spice and herb shop at Kloveniersburgwal 12.

Cheeses

Edam and Gouda are close by (*see pages 160 and 161*) so it's easy to buy from source. In Amsterdam try the Saturday market on the Lindengracht, or perhaps **Wout Arxhoex** at Damstraat 23, who have a very good selection of Dutch cheeses, over and above the usual Edam and Gouda types.

Drinks

There's nothing more *Oud Holland* than a stoneware bottle of *Oud Jenever,* which you can get at any good off-licence. If you want to go one better try **H P de Vreng En Zonen** at Nieuwendijk 75.

Ethnic/world artefacts

Amsterdam continues its tradition as a world market-place for exotic goods. A few of the more interesting specialist shops and galleries are **Italiaander Galleries** (African art), Prinsengracht 526; **Aboriginal Art and Instruments,** Spuistraat 183b; **Mikinook Tribal Art** (north of North America), Singel 190; **Kashba** (jewellery, art and furnishings), Staalstraat 3; **Imported** (Indonesia), Reestraat 12; **Terra** (Spanish ceramics and furniture), Reestraat 21; **M C Lennan's** (silks from India, China, Thailand), Hartenstraat 22; **Fanous Ramadan** (oriental lamps and lanterns), Runstraat 33.

See also the Tropenmuseum shop (*see pages 142–143*), which has some genuine high-quality artefacts on sale alongside the usual museum reproductions. For a wide choice of ethnic/New Age goods under one roof go to the basement of OIBIBIO (*see page 39*).

Flowers

If you want to take home some tulips, or any other flowers from Amsterdam, the **Bloemenmarkt** is probably your best bet. It has a huge range of bulbs for sale, though do make sure you get a certificate to clear customs, if one is required by your country. Another good place is the **Monday Plantenmarkt** at Amstelveld, next to the Amstelkerk.

Don't wait until you reach the airport to purchase flowers as the choice there is limited and expensive.

Typically Dutch

Blue delft-style miniatures, wooden tulips, pottery windmills and other Dutch *kitsch* can be found in any souvenir shop. For a comprehensive choice of high quality souvenirs try **De Bijenkorf**, Amsterdam's main department store, on Dam.

For delftware in Amsterdam go to **Focke & Meltzer** on P C Hoofstraat, **Rinascimento Gallerie d'Arte** at Prinsengracht 170 or **De Munt** in the Munttoren (*see page 32*). For delftware at source go to **De Porceleyne Fleys** in Delft, just half an hour south of Amsterdam (*see page 160*).

De Klompenboer on Nieuwezijds Voorburgwal (*see page 40*) make clogs on the premises. **'t Klompenhuis**, Nieuwe Hoogstraat 9 is the other city specialist. Both shops sells clogs to be worn as everyday footware as well as for tourist souvenirs.

Ultra-specialist

Among the many favourite one-product or single-category shops in Amsterdam are: **Het Condomerie**, Warmoesstraat (*see page 56*), devoted to condoms; **De Witten Tanden Winkel** (The White Teeth Shop), Runstraat, which features a surreal window display of cute little bendy toothbrushes on a ferris wheel; **Marañon**, on Singel, next to the Bloemenmarkt, which claims one of the largest collection of hammocks in the world; **Waterwinkel**, Roelof Hartstraat, which stocks over 100 types of bottled mineral water from all over the world; and **Christmas World** on Nieuwezijds Voorburgwal, behind the Nieuwe Kerk, which provides festive winter cheer all year round.

Amsterdam with children

Amsterdam is not the best city to bring young children to, though older ones will no doubt enjoy the novelty of a place where the main thoroughfares are waterways and many of the houses are straight from their history books.

Young children

A pushchair is a definite no-no. With narrow pavements, cobbles, narrow doors, stairways, and the need to hop on and hop off crowded trams, this is the last thing you, or your child, needs.

Eating out

Children are welcome in most eating establishments by day. By night most brown cafés are smoky places suitable only for adults, though in summer often you can sit at tables outside.

Without a doubt the most interesting children's eating place in the city is the **Kinder Kookcafe** (*Oudezijds Achterburgwal. Tel: 625 3257*). Its location in the Red-Light District is less than appetising, but its great novelty is that it serves meals for kids cooked by kids (aged 6–12, under adult supervision).

Youngsters are particularly welcome in the city's **pancake houses** (*see page 59*).

For snacking, kids probably won't like raw herring but chips and apple pie should go down a treat!

Good places for kids

Canal trip

Make sure they get a window seat. If you're feeling energetic you can pedal your own Canal Bike (*see page 16*).

Anne Frank House

An invaluable history lesson for older children, this is unsuitable for young ones – and there are long queues (*see pages 68–69*).

Artis Zoo

Take a safari in the city with all the usual favourites, plus rides and baby animals (*see pages 132–133*).

Nederlands Scheepvaartmuseum

Enquire at the desk about special children's activities. A visit aboard the 17th-century full-size replica

Amsterdam may well be the highlight of the whole trip. Make sure little ones have their hands tightly over their ears when the cannons are fired, though (*see pages 138–139*).

newMetropolis

This hands-on science centre is the answer to a parent's rainy day prayers. Salvation doesn't come cheap, though (*see pages 140–141*).

Tropenmuseum

The Tropical Museum is a big place, but if you're selective then young ones should find plenty of exhibits to interest them (*see pages 142–143*).

Vondelpark (in summer)

Let off steam without fear of trams or bikes and enjoy the buskers (*see pages 100–101*).

If all else fails try **Madame Tussaud's** (*see page 31*) or the **Holland Experience** (*see page 114*).

Good excursions

Amsterdamse Bos, particularly if they can ride a bike (*see page 150*); **Edam** for colour and cheesy razzmatazz (*see page 160*); **Scheveningen** for its beach and **Madurodam** – Holland in miniature (*see page 158*); **Zaanse Schans** for the last word in windmills (*see page 159*).

Bad places for kids

Unless you're the particularly liberal type the Red-Light District is not a good idea. Nor are most of the historical museums, houses and art galleries unless your child is a budding artist. Cat lovers should make an exception for the **Kattenkabinet** (*see page 90*) and you may, just, be able to drag them around part of the Rijksmuseum on the promise of its two exquisite dolls' houses (*see page 96*).

173

After dark

Britain has its pubs, Amsterdam has its brown cafés (also called brown bars). Brown refers to the colour of the ceiling and possibly walls, stained by decades of cigarette smoke. The oldest establishments date from the early 17th century.

Brown cafés

At its simplest a brown bar or café is a small drinking den, with bare wooden floorboards, perhaps sprinkled with sand to mop up the beer and whatever else is spilled, and wood-panelled walls. Some have faded squares of Turkish-style rugs on the tables which soak up spilled drink like giant beer mats.

In addition to serving alcoholic drinks brown cafés traditionally offer coffee and a limited variety of snacks (sausage, cheese etc) at lunchtime. However, in today's food-conscious times most are now turning themselves into *'eetcafés'* (ie putting the emphasis on food), and some have menus that are the equal of many restaurants.

Coffee shops

You can get an ordinary coffee here but it's cannabis, hash and marijuana that are the stock-in-trade of an Amsterdam coffee shop, and the cake on sale is probably the space-cake variety, baked with hashish. To make it absolutely obvious some of these establishments call themselves 'smoking coffee shops', but rather more of a giveaway are the trademark psychedelic or rastafarian décor, thumping music, sweet-smelling fumes and the customers draped over the chairs.

Just as selling or soliciting your body is technically illegal in Amsterdam, so is selling drugs; the customer must therefore approach the counter and ask for a menu.

If you do want to try smoking and you haven't done so before then find a place where the staff are knowledgeable and friendly and will give advice. Remember, as a general rule, that the blonde hash is lighter on your system than the black hash and that marijuana made in the Netherlands is usually the strongest variety. Staff are used to dealing with tourists and foreign visitors as they make up the majority of coffee shop visitors.

Rookies (Korte Leidsedwarsstraat) by Leidseplein and **The Grey Area** (Oude Leliestraat) in the Jordaan have a good name. Rookies is also one of the few coffee shops that is licensed to sell alcohol. The ubiquitous **Bulldog** chain has a good reputation for the quality of its soft drugs, but their outlets are far from the most pleasant or relaxed of places. It is best to avoid coffee shops in the Red-Light District, at least until you know what you are doing.

Some tourists think it is a good idea to take their video cameras into coffee shops, presumably to show the folks back home just how debauched the city is. As a result many establishments now have No Video Cameras signs on the doors.

Note that the city's tolerance of soft drugs does not extend to the hard stuff, such as speed, cocaine, ecstasy, LSD and heroin. If you are caught with any of these you will be prosecuted.

Mainstream performing arts

While the Netherlands does not have a great tradition in the performing arts, Amsterdam is a buzzing city attracting many of the best national and international theatre troupes, dancers and concert performers. In all there are around 15,000 concerts and shows per year.

The principal venues are the controversial **Muziektheater** (*see page 120*), the acclaimed **Concertgebouw** (*see page 86*), the **Beurs van Berlage** (*see page 27*) and the **Koninklijk Theater Carré** (*see page 114*). A performance at any of these venues is likely to be memorable.

Live bands

The famed multimedia centres of the **Melkweg** and the **Paradiso** (*see page 105*) are still the tops when it comes to attracting top-quality international acts who are happy to play smaller venues. You'll also catch excellent world music (and much more) at these places. A third multimedia centre, with a much smaller programme but still worth a look, is the **Arena**, to the east of the centre at 's'Gravensandestraat 51 (*Tram 6, 10. Tel: 694 7444*).

Another fashionable venue in tune with the multimedia ethos is **De Westergasfabriek** at Haarlemmerweg 8–10. Even if there is no event on, its trendy music café **West Pacific** is open daily from 1130 till late for eating, drinking and dancing.

Look out for big rock artists out of town at the huge **ArenA stadium** (note the final capital A). This is the home of the mighty Ajax Football Club – and should not be confused with the Arena multimedia centre (*see above*).

Nightclubs

In general, the nightlife around Rembrandtsplein and Leidseplein is pretty crass, so get down to Reguliersdwaarsstraat around midnight for a much classier selection, or brush up on your entrance lines and try to cross the portals of the ultra-trendy twosome, **Roxy** (*see page 41*) and **iT** (*see page 124*).

A peculiar Amsterdam night-clubbing custom is to tip the doorman as you leave the club (around f5). Obviously you only need do this if you want to return, but there's no guarantee that he'll be on the door next time you come, or even remember you – though no doubt he will do if you do not tip, and he certainly won't let you back in!

Jazz

The city has a long jazz tradition, which is most easily experienced at three lively, likeable little jazz-and-blues clubs either side of Leidseplein; Café Alto, Bamboo Bar (*see page 104*) and Bourbon Street (*see page 105*). If you can click your fingers in 13/14 time and dress like a beatnik try the Bimhuis (*see page 125*).

Film

Amsterdam is a film buff's town. No one should miss the magnificent Tuschinski Theater (*see page 121*) and serious filmgoers should check out the Filmmuseum in Vondelpark (*see page 105*) and The Movies on Haarlemmerdijk (*see page 77*).

What's On

For information on all arts and cultural events go to the Amsterdam Uitburo (AUB) in the Stadsschouwburg on Leidseplein (*Open Mon–Sat 1000–1800, Thur until 2100. Web site: www.aub.nl, e-mail: aub@aub.nl*).

What's On in Amsterdam is the official VVV monthly listings magazine. It's on sale in the VVV offices, although your hotel may well be able to supply you with a free copy.

For online information *Time Out* updates its entertainment pages weekly on *www.timeout.nl* (for more online information *see page 184*).

177

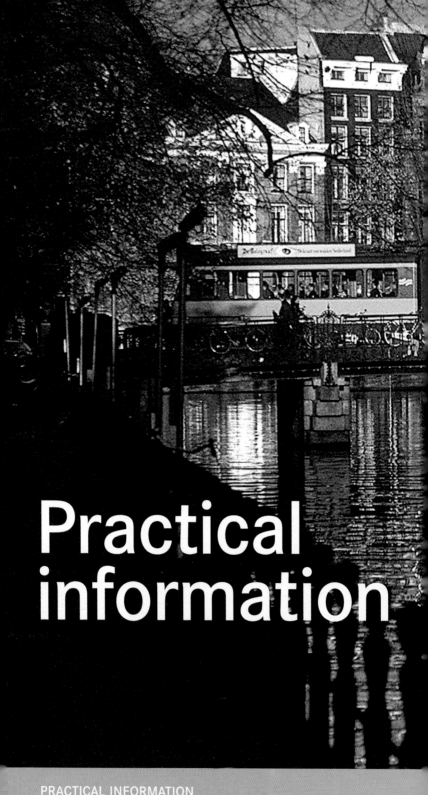

Practical
information

PRACTICAL INFORMATION

Practical information

Airport

Amsterdam's international airport is Schiphol, 14kms southwest of the city centre. It is a modern, efficient gateway, well signposted, with information and accommodation booking desks, bureaux de change and a good selection of shops.

Within the airport complex is the train station, with a fast and frequent service to the city centre. If you are staying close to the centre of town you will want to take the line to Amsterdam Centraal Station (CS). If you are staying to the south, perhaps in the Museum Quarter (Zuid WTC), you may be better off taking the line to the World Trade Centre, then catching the No 5 tram. (If you choose this option, buy a *strippenkaart* at the ticket desk, *see pages 15–16*). Enquire at the travel information desk for advice.

A very comfortable door-to-door service is provided by the KLM Airport Hotel shuttle bus, which runs between the airport and several city-centre hotels every 30-60 minutes. Despite the name, it is not reserved for KLM airline passengers and is available to anyone. It is a lot more expensive than rail and tram, but cheaper than a taxi and convenient if you have a lot of luggage.

Climate

The Netherlands is not noted for its hospitable climate and you should be prepared for the worst at most times of the year. It can rain at any time and in winter it does so frequently. From May to August temperatures average around 22°C, though the nights are cool and you will need a sweater or light jacket. In winter, chill winds off the North Sea blow along the canals, so wrap up warmly.

You can probably leave your ice skates at home; the picture-postcard scene of frozen canals occurs only once a decade or so.

Currency

The Dutch unit of currency is the guilder, also referred to as the florin. Abroad it is indicated as NLG, but is most commonly abbreviated in Holland as f (you may also see it referred to as fl, Hfl and Dfl). Notes are in denominations of f10, f25, f50, f100, f250 and f1000. The guilder is divided into 100 cents (c) and coins come in 5c, 10c, 25c, 100c (f1), 250c (f2.5) and 500c (f5).

Change your money at banks or bureaux de change. The former generally offer the best rates, but the latter are open longer hours. Shop around and don't be swayed by 'no commission' signs as this usually means a lower rate of exchange.

Customs regulations

EU nationals can import virtually any amount of alcohol, perfume, goods etc as long as it is for personal use. The import of meat products, fruit, flowers and protected animals is illegal.

Visitors from countries outside the EU can bring in 200 cigarettes, 50 cigars or 250gms tobacco; 1 litre of spirits or 2 litres of fortified wine or 2 litres of non-sparkling wine; a small amount of tea and coffee, and other goods to the value of f380.

Disabled travellers

With its cobbled streets, inaccessible trams, narrow broken pavements, narrow doorways, narrow stairs and lack of lifts the city can be a nightmare for wheelchair users. This does not mean it is out of the question, however.

Most museums have facilities for disabled travellers, there is a taxi service for wheelchair users (tel: 633 3943) and with careful planning and a strong and willing helper a good itinerary can still be put together.

Contact the tourist office for a leaflet detailing boat excursions, museums and other tourist attractions with facilities for disabled travellers.

Electricity

220 volts continental 2-pin round style plugs. Non-continental appliances will require an adaptor.

Entry formalities

If you are an EU national or from Australia, Canada, New Zealand or the USA you need only a valid passport to stay up to three months. Visitors from other countries should apply for a visa from their own country.

181

Festivals

Koninginnedag (*Queen's Day*) on 30 April is the big event in the Dutch calendar and celebrates the Queen's official birthday. It began as a children's festival, when kids would set up stalls selling sweets, cakes, toys and whatever. Now most adults get in on the act with an extra 2.5 million visitors from all over Holland cramming into Amsterdam to turn the city into one big street market and booze-fuelled party. The buskers come out in force, professional bands of all persuasions play on outdoor stages and partying starts early evening on the 29th. Top locations are Vondelpark and Leidseplein.

The Holland Festival, which runs throughout June, has been called Amsterdam's answer to the (mainstream) Edinburgh Festival. It features international dance, ballet, theatre, classical music and opera performances in venues all over town.

In July the **Summer Festival** is the fringe's answer to the Holland Festival.

The Uitmarkt (literally Entertainment Market) takes place on the last weekend in August and is a free trailer for forthcoming events in Holland's cultural calendar. Its activities centre round Dam.

On the first Saturday of September the annual **Bloemen Corso** (Flower Parade) takes place. Here you'll see and smell everything but tulips from Amsterdam (they're out of season). It starts and finishes outside town at Aalsmeer, but passes through various central city points.

Jordaan Festival takes place in mid-September.

Two festivals that have no traditional link with Amsterdam but are none the less celebrated with much gusto are New Year's Eve and Carnival (usually February). The former is a binge of booze and fireworks – be very careful as safety regulations vary between lax and non-existent; the latter an excuse for dressing ridiculously, parading and, once again, getting horribly drunk.

Health

EU countries have reciprocal medical treatment so in theory you should be able to recoup the cost of any medical care. However, this is a bureaucratic and time-wasting process so you are recommended always to carry adequate travel insurance.

For minor problems go to the nearest chemist (*drogist*), but for more serious matters involving prescription drugs you will need an *apotheek* (*open Mon–Fri 0830–1730*). Late- and weekend-opening branches are posted in the shop window. Call the English-speaking Central Doctors Service (*tel: 0900–503 2042, open 24 hrs*) for general advice or a referral to the nearest GP, dentist or chemist. In an emergency tel: 112.

One health hazard that you may not be aware of in these northern climes is mosquitoes (though they are non-malarial). In summer they breed in stagnant parts of the canals and if you are staying anywhere near the water then it's as well to take precautions.

Information

The Dutch tourist office is known as the VVV (pronounced *fay fay fay*). Staff are invariably knowledgeable, helpful and speak impeccable English. There are two tourist information offices at Centraal Station; the main office is opposite the main entrance on Stationsplein *(open daily 0900–1700)*, the other is inside the station on platform 2 *(open Mon–Sat 0800–1930, Sun 0900–1630)*. There is another on the corner of Leidsestraat and Leidseplein *(open Mon–Sat 0900–1900, Sun 0900–1700)*, and a less conveniently placed office south of the city centre at Stadionplein *(open Mon–Sat 0900–1700)*.

All offices will book accommodation (for a small fee plus a refundable deposit), change money and sell tickets for various events and excursions. None of the offices have a public telephone number, though there is a premium-rate recorded information line which is open 24 hours *(tel: 0900–400 4040 or 06 340 340 66)*.

There's also the Dutch Tourist Information Office at Damrak 35 *(tel: 638 2800, open Mon–Sat 0800–2200, Sun 0900–2200)* and the Holland Tourist Promotion office inside the airport at Schiphol Plaza *(open daily 0700–2200)*.

Netherlands Tourist Information Offices abroad:

Canada: 25 Adelaide Street East. Suite 710, Toronto, Ontario M5C 1Y2. Tel: 416/363 1577.

UK: 18 Buckingham Gate, London SW1E 6LD. Tel: 0171 828 7900; office open 1300-1500 for personal callers, tel: 0891 717 777 (premium-rate line).

USA: New York. 355 Lexington Avenue 21st Floor, New York NY 10017. Tel: 212/370 7367.

Chicago. 225 N Michigan Avenue, Suite 326, Chicago, IL 60601. Tel: 312/819 0300.

San Francisco. 605 Market Street, Room 401, San Francisco CA 94105. Tel: 415/543 6772.

Online

For on-line information there are two
main sites: *www.nbt.nl/nbt-amst-
index.html* and *www.amsterdam.nl*

Once in the city you can plug in
at several cafés, including De
Waag (Nieuwmarkt), Cyber Café
(Nieuwendijk 19) and Freeworld
(Nieuwendijk 30).

Note, too, the highly innovative pay-
and-surf public terminals (similar to
public telephones) dotted around the
centre of town. They are silver
coloured, marked KPN, and can be
found at Stationsplein (opposite

Centraal Station), Leidseplein, Paulus
Potterstraat (by the Stedelijk Museum)
and Spui, as well as at newMetropolis
and various cafés. These terminals
accept only payphone cards and are
much more expensive than surfing at
home. They cannot send e-mail but do
give print-outs.

If you have got your own machine
then you will need a four-pin phone
plug adaptor.

For the young-
at-heart

Pro-Amsterdam is a novel form of
word-of-mouth tourist information run

by the staff of the **Boom Chicago** comedy troupe (*see page 104*), at Leidseplein 12 (*open daily Apr–Sept 1200–1700*). They will advise you where to go for the best nightlife and the best restaurants. The service is free but tips are always welcome. Pick up their free house magazine, *Boom!,* which is full of useful information and tips.

Insurance

There are no special considerations for travel or holiday insurance in Amsterdam. If you lose property or are a victim of theft, report it to the nearest police station in order to get the documentation you will need for your own insurance claim purposes.

Language

English is the service language of Amsterdam and you need never ask anyone 'do you speak English' (unless they are very old, very young or you are well off the beaten track). The best convention is to give a cheerful *dag* (*dargh*, meaning hello) and then launch into whatever you want to say in English. None the less, as a guest in the Netherlands it's good manners to learn a few words and phrases:

185

hello/bye
dag (dargh)

goodbye/see you later
tot ziens (tot zeens)

yes
ja (yah)

no
ne (nay)

thank you/thanks
dank u (dank oo)/bedankt

excuse me
pardon (par-don)

cheers!
proost! (prorst)

It's also good to know the
difference between pull
(*trekken*) and push (*duwen*)
and open (*open*) and closed
(*gesloten/dicht*).

Maps

Falk publish several good
maps, available at the VVV,
most bookshops and some
souvenir shops.

Opening times

Shops: traditional hours are
Mon 1300–1800; Tue, Wed, Fri
0900–1800; Thur 0900–2100;
Sat 0900–1700. In the centre
of town many shops now also
open Sun from 1200–1700.

Banks: Mon–Fri 0900–1600.

Tourist Offices: (see Information,
page 183).

Businesses: Mon–Fri 0900–1700.

Bars: Sun–Thur from around
10/1100–0100, Fri and Sat until 0200.

Restaurants: traditional restaurants
hours are from around noon to
1400/1500, then again from 1700–2300,
with last orders around 2200. They
may be closed Sun and/or Mon.
Informal eating places tend to open
throughout the day, possibly all week,
though most still close around 2300.

Churches: most churches are only
open for services.

Museums: opening hours are
generally 1000–1800. Several museums
close on Mondays and public holidays.

Passes

The *Museum Jaarkaart* (Museum Yearcard) offers reduced or free admission to nearly 400 museums throughout the country.

A better bet for less museum-minded visitors is the *Amsterdam Culture & Leisure Pass,* which offers 31 free and discounted coupons for all sorts of leisure activities. The free entrance coupons to the Rijksmuseum (or Van Gogh Museum), Stedelijk Museum, Historical Museum and Rembrandthuis alone pay for the pass.

Passes are available from any tourist office and many hotels.

Public holidays

1 January

Good Friday

Easter Sunday and Monday

30 April Koninginnedag

5 May Remembrance Day

Ascension Day

Whit Sunday and Monday

25 and 26 December

For festivals (*see page 182*).

Reading

History
The Diary of a Young Girl/The Diary of Anne Frank/The Diaries of Anne Frank, Anne Frank. Essential reading to get a feeling for the atmosphere of Holland under the Nazis (*see pages 80–81*). **Note:** various editions of this world-famous book have been published with slightly different variations. Unless you have a scholarly interest it is not important which version you choose. For the best selection and advice buy from the shop in the Anne Frank House or visit the website: www.annefrank.nl.

Anne Frank Remembered, Miep Gies and Alison Leslie Gold (Corgi, 1988). An excellent companion book to the famous Diary, told from the viewpoint of Anne's most famous helper, Miep Gies.

Transatlantic Sketches, Henry James (1875). Amsterdam (among other places) as it was a century ago, through the inveterate American traveller's eyes.

Fiction
A Widow for One Year, John Irving, (1998). Mostly set in the Red-Light District.

Art
Dutch Painting, R H Fuchs (Thames & Hudson World of Art Series, 1978). A good guide to the history of Dutch art.

Lust for Life, Irving Stone (Methuen / N A L Dutton). The highly readable story of the tormented genius Vincent Van Gogh.

Safety and security

Amsterdam has a poor reputation for petty crime, particularly in the summer months when gangs of professional pickpockets make their way to the city to prey on unwary tourists. Beware of all approaches from strangers – the old favourite being the man who offers to wipe something off your jacket. Whatever the *modus operandi*, the aim is to distract your attention, if only for a split second, during which your wallet, bag or camera may be snatched by an accomplice. Be especially wary in crowded streets, on trams, busy squares and markets.

Violent crime against the tourist is unusual but beware of places where drug addicts hang out, notably parks after dark and the sleazy side-streets of the Red-Light District. If you stick to the main canalside streets in this quarter you should have no problems. Also in the Red-Light District don't take photographs of the window girls or your camera may end up in the canal.

Car and bicycle theft are popular city pastimes. Make sure your car is parked in a supervised parking area with absolutely nothing left inside it and if you are cycling never leave your bicycle unattended without locking it first.

Emergencies

In an emergency, tel: 112 for police, ambulance and fire brigade. The main police station is at Elandsgracht 117, tel: 559 9111

Telephones

International calls can be made from any public phone box. Most take phonecards, available from post

offices, tourist offices, stations and tobacconists. Many phones also take credit cards.

Off-peak rates are Mon–Fri 2000–0800 and all weekend.

Useful numbers

Amsterdam code **020**

Local and international operator **0800 0410** (free)

Directory Enquiries (Netherlands) tel: **0900 8008**

Directory Enquiries (overseas) tel: **0900 8418**

AT&T Direct tel: **0800–022 9111**

Time

Amsterdam is on Central European Time (CET). Now that the Spring and Autumn time changes have been synchronised this is always one hour ahead of Greenwich Mean Time (GMT).

Tipping

Unlike some countries, tipping is not ingrained into the service mentality and in most cases is not necessary. If the service has been good in a restaurant round the bill up to the nearest f5. Note, too, the unusual system of tipping bouncers upon leaving a nightclub (*see pages 176–177*).

Toilets

Amsterdam's only public toilets are its ancient green *pissoirs*. Quaint street furniture they may be, but they afford little privacy, dignity or hygiene, they smell absolutely disgusting and are few and far between. The alternative is the nearest café. Politeness dictates that you buy a drink but this is usually no hardship.

In semi-public places, such as museums and stations, there may be an attendant sitting outside the toilet. Pay the posted price or around 50 cents if it is left to your discretion. Ask for change if there is none on the plate.

189

Index

must-see AMSTERDAM
Editorial, design and production credits

Project management: Dial House Publishing Services
Series editor: Christopher Catling
Copy editor: Posy Gosling
Proof-reader: Susie Whimster

Series and cover design: Trickett & Webb Limited
Cover artwork: Wenham Arts
Text layout: Wenham Arts
Map work: RJS Associates

Repro and image setting: Z2 Repro, Thetford, Norfolk, UK
Printed and bound by: Artes Graficas ELKAR S. Coop., Bilbao, Spain

We would like to thank the following photographers for the loan of the
photographs reproduced in this book, to whom the copyright in the
photographs belongs:

Paul Murphy: pages 6, 7, 8, 9, 10, 11, 12, 13, 14, 15, 16, 17, 19, 20, 42, 43A, 43B,
53, 56B, 63, 68, 70A, 73A, 73B, 74, 75, 80, 82, 88, 91, 96, 108, 113, 120, 126, 134,
136, 138, 140, 146, 147, 150, 152, 154, 157, 160, 165, 166, 167, 168, 170, 171, 172,
174, 178, 181, 183, 186 and 188.

Eddy Posthuma de Boer: pages 4, 25, 26, 27, 28, 29, 31A, 31B, 32A, 32B, 34,
44, 49, 50, 51, 52, 54, 55, 56A, 62, 64, 70B, 72, 81, 86, 87, 90, 92, 94, 98, 100, 106,
112, 115, 116, 118, 119, 121, 127, 128, 132, 137, 142, 148, 157, 159, 162, 164, 175,
176, 180 and 184.

Picture research: Deborah Emeny